D1005850

THE NORMAL CHRISTIAN LIFE

HENDRICKSON CHRISTIAN CLASSICS

Anonymous, *The Kneeling Christian*

St. Augustine, *The Confessions*

E. M. Bounds, *E. M. Bounds on Prayer*

John Bunyan, *Grace Abounding to the Chief of Sinners*

John Bunyan, *The Pilgrim's Progress*

Gilbert Keith Chesterton, *Heretics*

Gilbert Keith Chesterton, *Orthodoxy*

John Foxe, *Foxe's Book of Martyrs*

Madame Guyon, *A Short Method of Prayer & Other Writings*

Thomas à Kempis, *The Imitation of Christ*

Abraham Kuyper, *Lectures on Calvinism*

Brother Lawrence, *The Practice of the Presence of God*

Andrew Murray, *Humility & Absolute Surrender*

Andrew Murray, *With Christ in the School of Prayer*

Watchman Nee, *The Normal Christian Life*

Charles Sheldon, *In His Steps*

Charles Haddon Spurgeon, *Morning by Morning*

R. A. Torrey, *How to Pray & How to Study the Bible*

A. W. Tozer, *Life in the Spirit*

John Wesley, *A Plain Account of Christian Perfection*

William Wilberforce, *A Practical View of Christianity*

THE NORMAL CHRISTIAN LIFE

WATCHMAN NEE

"IT IS NO LONGER I . . . BUT CHRIST"

HENDRICKSON
Christian
Classics

HENDRICKSON
PUBLISHERS

The Normal Christian Life

Hendrickson Publishers, Inc.
P. O. Box 3473
Peabody, Massachusetts 01961-3473

ISBN: 978-1-56563-456-5

The edition issued by special arrangement with Kingsway Publications, Lottbridge Drove, Eastbourne, East Sussex, England, BN23 6NT. Original title: *The Normal Christian Life*

Printed in the United States of America

Fifth Printing — November 2010

Scripture quotations are from the 1881 (English) Revised Version (RV) of the King James Bible unless otherwise indicated, not to be confused with the later RSV (Revised Standard Version, 1946).

In Bible references, marginal readings (alternate translations) are indicated by "marg." after the reference.

CONTENTS

Preface

Hendrickson Christian Classics Edition

Watchman Nee, born as Ni Shu-tsu (Henry Nee)
1903-1972

Leadership and charismatic presence. Solid teaching content. A means for disseminating the message beyond a local audience. These are key aspects of regional church leaders whose writings become world-renowned classics. And such a man was Watchman Nee, born as Ni Shu-tsu (Henry Nee) in 1903 on the southeastern coast of China, north of Hong Kong.

Like so many of us, Nee had a Christian heritage. His paternal grandfather, baptized in 1857, had been an ordained Congregational pastor. His maternal grandparents halted their adoptive daughter's plans to go to medical school in the States and arranged instead for her to marry their pastor's son, Ni Weng-hsiu.

One dark night during her third pregnancy—after birthing two daughters—Mrs. Ni prayed desperately for a son, like the biblical Hannah, committing him to the Lord's service. As she lay awake, she heard the town watchman walking the streets; years later memory of that desperate night-time prayer prompted her to suggest her son's baptismal name: To-sheng, or "Watchman."

Over the years, Watchman's domineering mother grew more interested in politics than in church. And young Watchman, though educated in Anglican schools, was disinterested in faith. But all this changed in 1920, when Mrs. Ni attended Methodist revival meetings featuring the preaching of Dora Yu, a woman Mrs. Ni had met briefly while in college. Influenced by the witness of two women—the preaching of Dora Yu and the spiritual transformation of his harsh mother—Watchman himself surrendered his life to Christ.

Watchmen never enrolled in university, but rather immersed himself in the Word, in the Christian community, and in evangelistic efforts. His ongoing Christian formation continued to come through the ministry and tutelage of women—an independent British missionary, Margaret Barber; Ruth Lee, through whose preaching he found the "full assurance of salvation"; the writings of Madame Guyon,[1] among others.

By time he was twenty, Watchman's leadership was evident. He was printing and distributing his sermons in a publication called *Revival* (later called *The Christian,* as its content became less evangelistic and focused more on discipleship training). With other young zealots, he was leading evangelistic forays. He was preaching and teaching in-depth biblical expositions. In his private time, he was voraciously reading church history and Western devotional and expositional books—and writing a major Bible curriculum, titled *The Spiritual Man,* explicating salvation in terms of the human spirit, soul, and body.

All this took its toll, and in Nee's mid-twenties doctors diagnosed potentially—probably—fatal tuberculosis. A hiatus of activity renewed his strength, but ultimately he felt he had been miraculously healed of the disease. During this rest, in 1927, he came to a new understanding of the message of Paul's Epistle to the Romans—an understanding that plays

---

[1] Madam Jeanne Marie Bouvier de la Mothe Guyon (1647–1717), a French Christian mystic, is best known as the author of *A Short and Easy Method of Prayer,* which, along with *Spiritual Torrents,* another of her well-known works, is available in a Hendrickson Christian Classic edition entitled *A Short Method of Prayer and Other Writings,* 2005.

largely in the content of *The Normal Christian Life*. Nee says of this experience,

> I asked God to show me what was the meaning of the expression "I have been crucified with Christ." It had become clear to me that when speaking of this subject God nowhere says "You must be," but always "You have been. . . ."
>
> All at once I *saw* my oneness with Christ: that I was in him, and that when he died I died. My death to sin was a matter of the past, and not of the future.[2]

The Spiritual Man, published in 1928, was the only book Nee set out to write—later books being compilations put together with or without his approval. And by the 1940s he distanced himself from this work, "not that what I wrote was wrong," he said, but that it was too rational and systematic.

> The danger of systematizing divine facts is that a man can understand without the help of the Holy Spirit. It is only the immature Christian who demands always to have intellectually satisfying conclusions. [3]

Nee would change other views in time. It was Westerners, not Chinese believers, who prompted him to question the role of women in ministry leadership. This is curious, since God had used female preachers and leaders to bring Watchman himself to Christ.

Westerners influenced his thinking, but so did a strong nationalism that churned among students in the mid-to-late 1920s. Nee remained fiercely independent from established mission boards or denominations. The schismatic nature of the Western church—some groups in disfellowship with others—fueled his vision for a church administrative structure, called the Little Flock movement, that relied on local "tent-maker" leadership, initially with loose regional administrative oversight.

The 1930s opened new vistas: in 1934 Watchman married a woman he'd known since childhood, Charity Change, the daughter of a Christian and Missionary Alliance pastor. Having a master's degree in English, Charity helped some with translation and in ministry, but generally out of

---

[2] *Against the Tide: The Story of Watchman Nee*, by Angus Kinnear (Fort Washington, Pa.: CLC Publications, 1973), formerly titled *Watchman Nee: Against the Tide*.

[3] *Ibid*, page 103.

the lime-light. Charity had one unsuccessful pregnancy, but the Nees never had any children.

In the thirties, Watchman made several trips to the West, principally in 1938, when he taught at the Keswick Convention[4] in England and went on to the Continent, where he gave the Denmark lectures that provide the backbone of *The Normal Christian Life*. Before he returned to occupied China in 1939, his book, *Rethinking the Work*, was published in England. In it he laid out his sometimes controversial "one locality, one church" view of church administration: that all believers in a certain neighborhood, town, or city should worship in one local congregation—as a Little Flock.

During the War, the financial hardships of the church prompted Nee to uncharacteristically embark on a pharmaceutical manufacturing enterprise, using any profits to support the work of the church. In retrospect, the whole venture seemed badly visioned and schismatic to the church. Rumors arose; the Shanghai congregation censured him, even as they sorely needed his presence and teaching. A leadership vacuum was filled by Watchman's more fiery and dogmatic friend, Witness Lee, who, after the War, drew Nee back from "exile."

In 1947, when Nee returned to a teaching-preaching ministry, his biographer notes, he "returned to his spiritual starting point, the foundation principles of his message of the Cross."[5] New lectures, published under the title *The Release of the Spirit*, "are concerned with the principle of 'brokenness' as a condition of the release of divine power."[6]

In this post-War era, revival was kindled, and the Little Flock leadership regrouped, now seeing new insight into the structure of the church based on a New Testament model. With evangelism in mind, bands of believers pooled resources, and some moved from the cities to the countryside, as the early church had gone forth from their base in Jerusalem.

---

[4] The Keswick Convention, which is still being held, is an important week-long religious gathering of evangelical Christians, and has been held annually at Keswick, England, since 1875. The Convention is chiefly "for the promotion of practical holiness" by means of prayer, discussion, and personal interaction.

[5] *Against the Tide.*

[6] *Ibid.*

Some resources were used to start businesses, which ultimately sniffed of capitalism to the communist revolutionaries looming in the political background. These shifts in the 1940s pulled the Little Flock movement toward a centrally controlled and authoritarian church structure that surprised many, as it seemed so far removed from Watchman's early vision of local church autonomy and a freedom of spirit.

Watchman had read Marx, and understood the threat of communism to the church, and yet he taught with a new vigor, writing and presenting weekly (fifty-two) systematic lessons on the basics of Christianity. The communists gained control in 1949 and began to infiltrate the church. However, they did not seriously crack down and demand allegiance to the state-run church, Three Self Patriotic Movement, for several years.

In 1952, the government required Watchman to go to Manchuria to settle issues regarding the pharmaceutical company, and from that trip he never returned home. Taken into police custody, he was held—and not heard from—until he was brought to trial in Shanghai in 1956. He was then found guilty of five counts, ranging from espionage and counterrevolutionary activities to licentious dissolution, and formally sentenced to fifteen years (some accounts say twenty) in prison, time being counted from his 1952 arrest.

His wife Charity was detained briefly in 1956 and released, living spartanly and isolated in Shanghai, until her death in 1971 from complications after a fall. After 1956, Charity was allowed an occasional visit to Watchman in a Shanghai prison, and he was allowed to write and receive a monthly letter.

Having served twenty years, Nee might have been near release from prison in 1972. However, on June 1, he died of unknown causes, still in custody, but at a facility inland, away from the city, in Anhwei Province. His biographer, Angus Kinnear, found no substantiation for Cold-War rumors (1970) that Nee had been physically mutilated by his captors. Some evidence: he was known to work as an English-to-Chinese translator of medical books. Charity's older sister visited him in the Shanghai prison after Charity's death and received a letter from him in April 1972, written in his distinct hand, saying, "I maintain my own joy." (Kinnear reminds us of censorship disallowing any mention of "God" in correspondence.)[7]

Sketchy reports from the Shanghai prison indicate that Watchman was an encouraging influence; even in isolation, he was heard singing hymns in the early morning, like Paul and Silas in another age.

And in those years of imprisonment, his written works—again, most compiled from sermons and lectures—gained prominence in the West. *The Normal Christian Life* is chief among these now-classic writings. Its teaching, primarily on Romans 1–8, is refreshing, grounded in scriptural texts (he read the entire New Testament once a month) and reminiscent of the quietism of Madame Guyon. But this is not a boring didactic or expositional treatise. Nee's pastoral acumen prompted him to pepper his talks with engaging, enlightening anecdotes that work across cultural and generational lines to draw the reader in. Nee's work also has served to remind the church in the free world to remember and pray for thousands of Christians worldwide who have been or are persecuted and detained for their faith and witness.

Significantly, as edited by Angus Kinnear in 1957, *The Normal Christian Life* ends with a chapter titled "The Goal of the Gospel."[8] It includes this startling commentary, prophetic of Nee's own final decades:

> We like to be always "on the go": the Lord would sometimes prefer to have us in prison. We think in terms of apostolic journeys: God dares to put His greatest ambassadors in chains.

He then quotes the apostle Paul:

> But thanks be unto God, which always leadeth us in triumph in Christ, and maketh manifest through us the savor of his knowledge in every place (2 Cor. 2:14).

---

[7] *Ibid.*

[8] This chapter begins on page 177.

Preface

to the First Edition (1957)

The author of these studies, Mr. Watchman Nee (Nee To-sheng) of Foochow, a true bondservant of Jesus Christ, placed a great many of us in his debt when, on a visit to Europe in 1938 and 1939, he set forth so lucidly in his ministry to many groups of young workers and others, the foundation principles of the Christian life and walk.

Several of the addresses forming the material from which this book has been compiled, have already been published independently, and have been the means of blessing to many. Others, covering similar but wider ground, have existed for long in manuscript or note form. It is with the conviction that their message merits a wider circulation at the present time that I have undertaken the editing of the available material to form this larger book.

Being deprived of personal contact or communication with the author, I have myself to take full responsibility for the work of editing. This has involved the bringing together of matter from a number of sources to form a logical sequence within the framework provided by two of the original series of studies. Due to the wide variety of this material, including verbatim records of spoken English addresses, private notes of Bible readings and personal conversations, and a few translations from the Chinese, liberties, perforce, have had to be taken with the literary arrangement—not, of course, with the doctrine—making the hand of the editor more evident that I would have wished. But the privilege of close personal contact with Mr. Nee during 1938, and the help and criticism of others who enjoyed his ministry or who have worked with him, and who knew him better than I, have combined, in the few places where interpretation was necessary, to make faithfulness to his thought the more certain.

Work on this book has been a searching experience. It goes out now with the prayer that its strong emphasis upon the greatness of Christ, and upon the finality and sufficiency of his work, may be used of God to bring His children to a place of greater spiritual effectiveness, and thus of increasing value to him.

Angus I. Kinnear, Editor
Bangalore, India, 1957

Preface

to the British Edition (1958)

A new edition has made possible further revision and occasional slight expansion of the text with the aid of fresh source material.

The reader is again reminded that the author's message in this collected form had its origin as spoken ministry. It is therefore not wholly systematic. On none of the subjects dealt with, is it to be regarded as exhaustive. It should be approached prayerfully—not as a treatise, but as a living message to the heart.

Angus I. Kinnear
1958

Preface

PREFACE

TO THE THIRD EDITION (1961)

The ministry of Watchman Nee had been known in English only from transcriptions of his spoken messages in tracts and magazine articles when, in 1957, *The Normal Christian Life* was first published in Bombay and was at once accorded a widespread welcome. complied from such records and from private notebooks, this collection was edited in the author's absence, and is based upon addresses originally given by Mr. Nee during and shortly after a visit to Europe in 1938–39.

From the day in 1920 when, as a college student, he found the Lord Jesus Christ as his Savior during the visit of a Chinese evangelist to his native city of Foochow, Nee To-sheng gave himself without reserve to God for work among his own people. Over the years he became widely known in China as a gifted preacher of the Gospel and an original expositor of the Word, whose ministry bore remarkable fruit in individuals and in many groups of spiritually virile Christians. This book sets forth something of his personal understanding of the Christian life toward s the end of those first year of unrestricted service for his Lord.

In the years that have followed, the Church of God in China has passed through recurring periods of the severest testing with bu brief interludes of respite, and the author, together with many of those associated with him in work and witness, has had his full share of these experiences right up to the present [1961]. It is perhaps not surprising therefore that his ministry should come to us today with freshness and power. Many have already testified to the transformation this book has wrought in their lives through new discoveries of the greatness of Christ and of His finished work on the cross.

The demand for a new edition made possible a further careful revision of the text in 1961. Readers are reminded that this is a compilation of spoken addresses and not, despite superficial appearances, a systematic treatise of Christian doctrine. It is to be approached not as an intellectual exercise but as a message to the heart. Read thus it will, I believe, speak as from the Spirit of God Himself, with challenging power.

Angus I. Kinnear
London, 1961

Chapter 1

The Blood of Christ

What is the *normal* Christian life? We do well at the outset to ponder this question. The object of these studies is to show that it is something very different from the life of the *average* Christian. Indeed, a consideration of the written Word of God—of the Sermon on the Mount, for example—should lead us to ask whether such a life has ever, in fact, been lived upon the earth, *save only by the Son of God himself.* But in that last saving clause lies immediately the answer to our question.

The Apostle Paul gives us his own definition of the Christian life in Galatians 2:20. It is "no longer I, but Christ." Here he is not stating something special or peculiar—a high level of Christianity. He is, we believe, presenting God's *normal* [state] for a Christian, which can be summarized in the words: I live no longer, but Christ lives his life in me.

God makes it quite clear in his Word that he has only one answer to every human need—his Son, Jesus Christ. In all his dealings with us, he works by taking *us* out of the way and substituting Christ in our place. The Son of God died instead of us for our forgiveness: he lives instead of us for our

1

deliverance. So we can speak of two substitutions—a Substitute on the Cross, who secures our forgiveness, and a Substitute within, who secures our victory. It will help us greatly, and save us from much confusion, if we keep constantly before us this fact, that God will answer all our questions in one way and one way only: namely, by showing us more of his Son.

Our Dual Problem: *Sins* and *Sin*

We shall take now as a starting-point for our study of the normal Christian life, that great exposition of it which we find in the first eight chapters of the Epistle to the Romans, and we shall approach our subject from a practical and experimental point of view. It will be helpful, first of all, to point out a natural division of this section of Romans into two, and to note certain striking differences in the subject-matter of its two parts.

The first eight chapters of Romans form a self-contained unit. The four and a half chapters from 1:1 to 5:11 form the first half of this unit, and the three and a half chapters from 5:12 to 8:39 the second half. A careful reading will show us that the subject-matter of the two halves is not the same. For example, in the argument of the first section, we find the plural word "sins" given prominence. In the second section, however, this changed, for, while the word "sins" hardly occurs once, the singular word "sin" is used again and again and is the subject mainly dealt with. Why is this?

It is because in the first section it is a question of the sins I have committed before God, which are many and can be enumerated, whereas in the second it is a question of sin as a principle working in me. No matter how many sins I commit, it is always the one sin principle that leads to them. I need forgiveness for my sins, but I need also deliverance from the power of sin. The former touches my conscience, the latter my life. I may receive forgiveness for all my sins, but because of my sin I have, even then, no abiding peace of mind.

When God's light first shines into my heart, my one cry is for forgiveness, for I realize I have committed sins before him; but when, once I have received forgiveness of *sins,* I make a new discovery, namely, the discovery of *sin,* and I realize not only that I have committed sins before God, but that there is something wrong within. I discover that I have the nature of a sinner. There is an inward inclination to sin, a power within that draws to sin. When that

2

power breaks out, I commit sins. I may seek and receive forgiveness, but then I sin once more. So life goes on in a vicious circle of sinning and being forgiven and then sinning again. I appreciate the blessed fact of God's forgiveness, but I want something more than that: I want deliverance. I need forgiveness for what I have *done,* but I need also deliverance from what I *am.*

God's Dual Remedy: The Blood and the Cross

Thus in the first eight chapters of Romans, two aspects of salvation are presented to us: firstly, the forgiveness of our sins, and secondly, our deliverance from sin. But now, in keeping with this fact, we must notice a further difference.

In the first part of Romans 1 to 8, we twice have reference to the Blood of the Lord Jesus: in chapter 3:25 and in chapter 5:9. In the second, a new idea is introduced in chapter 6:6, where we are said to have been "crucified" with Christ. The argument of the first part gathers round that aspect of the work of the Lord Jesus which is represented by "the Blood" shed for our justification through "the remission of sins." This terminology is, however, not carried on into the second section, where the argument centers now in the aspect of his work represented by "the Cross," that is to say, by our union with Christ in his death, burial and resurrection. This distinction is a valuable one. We shall see that the Blood deals with what we have done, whereas the Cross deals with what we are. The Blood disposes of our sins, while the Cross strikes at the root of our capacity for sin. The latter aspect will be the subject of our consideration in later chapters.

The Problem of Our Sins

We begin, then, with the precious Blood of the Lord Jesus Christ and its value to us in dealing with our sins and justifying us in the sight of God. This is set forth for us in the following passages:

All have sinned (Romans 3:23).

God commendeth his own love toward us, in that, while we were yet sinners, Christ died for us. Much more then, being now justified by his blood, shall we be saved from the wrath of God through him (Romans 5:8–9).

Being justified freely by his grace through the redemption that is in Christ Jesus: whom God set forth to be a propitiation, through faith, by

3

his blood, to shew his righteousness, because of the passing over of the sins done aforetime, in the forbearance of God; for the shewing, I say, of his righteousness at this present season: that he might himself be just, and the justifier of him that hath faith in Jesus (Romans 3:24–26).

We shall have reason at a later stage in our study to look closely at the real nature of the fall and the way of recovery. At this point we will just remind ourselves that when sin came in, it found expression in an act of disobedience to God (Romans 5:19). Now we must remember that whenever this occurs, the thing that immediately follows, is guilt.

Sin enters as disobedience, to create first of all a separation between God and man, whereby man is put away from God. God can no longer have fellowship with him, for there is something now which hinders, and it is that which is known throughout Scripture as "sin." Thus it is first of all God who says, "They are all under sin" (Romans 3:9). Then, secondly, that sin in man, which henceforth constitutes a barrier to his fellowship with God, gives rise in him to a sense of guilt—of estrangement from God. Here it is man himself who, with the help of his awakened conscience, says, "I have sinned" (Luke 15:18). Nor is this all, for sin also provides Satan with his grounds for accusation before God, while our sense of guilt gives him his grounds for accusation in our hearts; so that, thirdly, it is "the accuser of the brethren" (Rev. 12:10) who now says, "You have sinned."

To redeem us, therefore, and to bring us back to the purpose of God, the Lord Jesus had to do something about these three questions: of sin, and of guilt, and of Satan's charge against us. Our sins had first to be dealt with, and this was effected by the precious Blood of Christ. Our guilt has to be dealt with and our guilty conscience set at rest by showing us the value of that Blood. And finally the attack of the enemy has to be met and his accusations answered. In the Scriptures the Blood of Christ is shown to operate effectually in these three ways: Godward, manward, and Satanward.

There is thus an absolute need for us to appropriate these values of the Blood if we are to go on. This is a first essential. We must have a basic knowledge of the fact of the death of the Lord Jesus as our Substitute upon the Cross, and a clear apprehension of the efficacy of his Blood for our sins, for without this, we cannot be said to have started upon our road. Let us look then at these three matters more closely.

The Blood Is Primarily for God

The Blood is for atonement and has to do first with our standing before God. We need forgiveness for the sins we have committed, lest we come under judgment; and they are forgiven, not because God overlooks what we have done, but because he sees the Blood. The Blood is therefore not primarily for us, but for God. If I want to understand the value of the Blood, I must accept God's valuation of it, and if I do not know something of the value set upon the Blood by God, I shall never know what its value is for me. It is only as the estimate that God puts upon the Blood of Christ is made known to me by his Holy Spirit, that I come into the good of it myself, and find how precious indeed the Blood is to me. But the first aspect of it is Godward. Throughout the Old and New Testaments the word "blood" is used in connection with the idea of atonement, I think over a hundred times, and throughout, it is something for God.

In the Old Testament calendar there is one day that has a great bearing on the matter of our sins, and that day is the Day of Atonement. Nothing explains this question of sins so clearly as the description of that day. In Leviticus 16, we find that on the Day of Atonement, the blood was taken from the sin offering and brought into the Most Holy Place, and there sprinkled before the Lord seven times. We must be very clear about this. On that day, the sin offering was offered publicly in the court of the tabernacle. Everything was there in full view and could be seen by all. But the Lord commanded that no man should enter the tabernacle itself except the high priest. It was he alone who took the blood and, going into the Most Holy Place, sprinkled it there to make atonement before the Lord. Why? Because the high priest was a type of the Lord Jesus in his redemptive work (Hebrews 9:11–12), and so, in figure, he was the one who did the work. None but he could even draw near to enter in. Moreover, connected with his going in, there was but one act, namely, the presenting of the blood to God as something he had accepted, something in which he could find satisfaction. It was a transaction between the high priest and God in the Sanctuary, away from the eyes of the men who were to benefit

5

by it. The Lord required that. The Blood is therefore, in the first place, not for ourselves, but for Him.

Earlier even than this there is described in Exodus 12:13 the shedding of the blood of the Passover lamb in Egypt for Israel's redemption. This is again, I think, one of the best types in the Old Testament of our redemption. The blood was put on the lintel and on the door-posts, whereas the meat, the flesh of the lamb, was eaten inside the house; and God said: "When I see the blood, I will pass over you." Here we have another illustration of the fact that the blood was not meant to be presented to man but to God, for the blood was put on the lintel and on the door-posts, where those feasting inside the house would not see it.

God Is Satisfied

It is God's holiness, God's righteousness, which demands that a sinless life should be given for man. There is life in the Blood, and that Blood has to be poured out for me, for my sins. God is the One who requires it to be so. God is the One who demands that the Blood be presented, in order to satisfy his own righteousness, and it is he who says: "*When I see the blood, I will pass over you.*" The Blood of Christ wholly satisfies God.

Now I desire to say a word at this point to my younger brethren in the Lord, for it is here that we often get into difficulties. As unbelievers we may have been wholly untroubled by our conscience until the Word of God began to arouse us. Our conscience was dead, and those with dead consciences are certainly of no use to God. But later, when we believed, our awakened conscience may have become acutely sensitive, and this can constitute a real problem to us. The sense of sin and guilt can become so great, so terrible, as almost to cripple us by causing us to lose sight of the true effectiveness of the Blood. It seems to us that our sins are so real, and some particular sin may trouble us so many times, that we come to the point where, to us, our sins loom larger than the Blood of Christ.

Now the whole trouble with us is that we are trying to sense it; we are trying to feel its value and to estimate subjectively what the Blood is for us. We cannot do it; it does not work that way. The Blood is first for God to see. We then have to accept God's valuation of it. In doing so, we shall find our salvation. If instead we try to come to a valuation by way of our feelings, we get nothing; we remain in darkness. No, it is a matter of faith in God's Word. We have to believe that the Blood is precious to God *because he says it is so* (1 Peter 1:18–19). If God can accept the Blood as a payment for our sins and as the price of our redemption, then we can rest assured that the debt has been paid. If God is satisfied with the Blood, then the Blood must be acceptable. Our valuation of it is only according to His valuation—neither more, nor less. It cannot, of course, be more, but it *must not* be less. Let us remember that he is holy and he is righteous, and that a holy and righteous God has the right to say that the Blood is acceptable in his eyes, and has fully satisfied him.

The Believer's Access to God

The Blood has satisfied God; it must satisfy us also. It has therefore a second value that is manward in the cleansing of our conscience. When we come to the Epistle to the Hebrews, we find that the Blood does this. We are to have "hearts sprinkled from an evil conscience" (Hebrews 10:22).

This is most important. Look carefully at what it says. The writer does not tell us that the Blood of the Lord Jesus cleanses our hearts, and then stop there in his statement. We are wrong to connect the heart with the Blood in quite that way. It may show a misunderstanding of the sphere in which the Blood operates to pray, "Lord, cleanse my heart from sin by thy Blood." The heart, God says, is "desperately sick" (Jeremiah 17:9), and he must do something more fundamental than cleanse it: he must give us a new one.

We do not wash and iron clothing that we are going to throw away. As we shall shortly see, the "flesh" is too bad to be cleansed; it must be crucified. The work of God within us must be something wholly new. "A new heart also will I give you, and a new spirit will I put within you" (Ezekiel 36:26).

No, I do not find it stated that the Blood cleanses our hearts. Its work is not subjective in that way, but wholly objective, before God. True, the cleansing work of the Blood is seen here in Hebrews 10, to have reference to the heart, but it is in relation to the conscience. "Having our hearts sprinkled from a evil conscience." What then is the meaning of this?

It means that there was something intervening between myself and God, as a result of which I had an evil conscience whenever I sought to approach him. It was constantly reminding me of the barrier that stood between myself and him. But now, through the operation of the precious Blood, something new has been effected before God which has removed that barrier, and God has made that fact known to me in his Word. When that has been believed in and accepted, my conscience is at once cleared and my sense of guilt removed, and I have no more an evil conscience toward God.

Every one of us knows what a precious thing it is to have a conscience void of offense in our dealings with God. A heart of faith and a conscience clear of any and every accusation are both equally essential to us, since they are interdependent. As soon as we find our conscience is uneasy, our faith leaks away, and immediately we know we cannot face God. In order therefore to keep going on with God we must know the up-to-date value of the Blood. God keeps short accounts, and we are made nigh by the Blood every day, every hour, and every minute. It never loses its efficacy as our grounds for access if we will but lay hold upon it. When we enter the most Holy Place, on what grounds dare we enter but by the Blood?

But I want to ask myself, am I really seeking the way into the Presence of God by the Blood, or by something else? What do I mean when I say, "by the Blood"? I mean simply that I recognize my sins, that I confess that I have need of cleansing and of atonement, and that I come to God on the basis of the finished work of the Lord Jesus. I approach God through his merit alone, and never on the basis of my attainment; never, for example, on the grounds that I have been extra kind or patient today, or that I have done something for the Lord this morning. I have to come by way of the Blood *every time*. The temptation to so many of us when we try to approach God is to think that, because God has been dealing with us—because he has been taking steps to bring us into something more of himself and has been teaching us deeper lessons of the Cross—he has thereby set before us new standards, and that only by attaining to these can we have a clear conscience before him. No! A clear conscience is *never* based upon our attainment; it can only be based on the work of the Lord Jesus in the shedding of his Blood.

I may be mistaken, but I feel very strongly that some of us are thinking in terms such as these: "Today I have been a little more careful; today I have been doing a little better; this morning I have been reading the Word of God in a warmer way, so today I can pray better!" Or again, "Today I have had a little difficulty with the family; I began the day feeling very gloomy and depressed; I am not feeling too bright now; it seems that there must be something wrong; therefore the way is not clear for me to approach God."

What, after all, is your basis of approach to God? Do you come to him on the uncertain ground of your feeling, the feeling that you may have achieved something for God today? Or is your approach based on something far more secure: namely, the fact that the Blood has been shed, and that God looks on that Blood and is satisfied? Of course, were it conceivably possible for the Blood to suffer any change, the basis of your approach to God might be less trustworthy. But the Blood has never changed and never will. Your approach to God is therefore always in boldness; and that boldness is yours through the Blood, and never through your personal attainment. Whatever be your measure of attainment today or yesterday or the day before, as soon as you make a conscious move into the Most Holy Place, immediately you have to take your stand upon the safe and only grounds of the shed Blood. Whether you have had a good day or a bad day, whether you have consciously sinned or not, your basis of approach is always the same—the Blood of Christ. God's acceptance of that Blood is the ground upon which you may enter, and there is no other.

As with many other stages of our Christian experience, this matter of access to God has two phases, an initial and a progressive one. The former is presented to us in Ephesians 2 and the latter in Hebrews 10. Initially, our standing with God was secured by the Blood, for we are "made nigh in the blood of Christ" (Eph. 2:13). But thereafter our grounds for continual access is still by the Blood, for the apostle exhorts us: "Having therefore . . . boldness to enter into the holy place by the blood of Jesus . . . let us draw near" (Heb. 10:19, 22). To begin with, I was made nigh by the Blood, and to continue in that new relationship, I come through the Blood every time. It is not that I was saved on one basis and that I now maintain my fellowship on another. You say, "That is very simple; it is the A.B.C. of the Gospel." Yes, but the trouble with many of us is that we have moved away from the A.B.C. We have thought we had progressed and so could dispense with it, but we can never do so. No, my initial approach to God is by the Blood, and every time I come before him it is the same. Right to the end, it will always and only be on the grounds of the precious Blood.

This does not mean at all that we should live a careless life, for we shall shortly study another aspect of the death of Christ which shows us that anything but that is contemplated. But for the present let us be satisfied with the Blood, that it is there and that it is enough.

We may be weak, but looking at our weakness will never make us strong. No trying to feel bad and doing penance will help us to be even a little holier. There is no help there, so let us be bold in our approach because of the Blood:

> Lord, I do not know fully what the value of the Blood is, but I know that the Blood has satisfied thee; so the Blood is enough for me, and it is my only plea. I see now that whether I have really progressed, whether I have really attained to something or not, is not the point. Whenever I come before thee, it is always on the grounds of the precious Blood.

Then our conscience is really clear before God. No conscience could ever be clear apart from the Blood. It is the Blood that gives us boldness.

"No more conscience of sins": these are tremendous words of Hebrews 10:2. We are cleansed from every sin; and we may truly, with Paul, echo the words of David: "Blessed is the man to whom the Lord will not reckon sin" (Romans 4:8).

Overcoming the Accuser

In view of what we have said, we can now turn to face the enemy, for there is a further aspect of the Blood which is Satanward. Satan's most strategic activity in this day is as the accuser of the brethren, (Rev. 12:10) and it is as this that our Lord confronts him with his special ministry as High Priest "through his own blood" (Hebrews 9:12).

How then does the Blood operate against Satan? It does so by putting God on the side of man against him. The Fall brought about a state of affairs in man which gave Satan a footing within him, with the result that God was compelled to withdraw himself. Man is now outside the garden—beyond reach of the glory of God (Romans 3:23)—because he is inwardly estranged from God. Because of what man has done, there is that in him now, which, until it is removed, renders God morally unable to defend him. But the Blood removes that barrier and restores man to God and God to man. Man is in favor now, and because God is on his side, he can face Satan without fear.

You remember that verse in John's first Epistle—and this is the translation of it I like best: "The blood of Jesus his Son cleanses us from *every* sin"[1] It is not exactly "all sin" in the general sense, but *every* sin, every item. What does it mean? Oh, it is a marvelous thing! God is the light, and as we walk in the light with him, everything is exposed and open to that light, so that God can see it all—*and yet* the Blood is able to cleanse from every sin. What a cleansing! It is not that I have not a profound knowledge of myself, nor that God has not a perfect knowledge of me. It is not that I try to hide something nor that God tries to overlook something. No, it is that he is in the light, and I too am in the light, and that *there,* the precious Blood cleanses me from every sin. The Blood is enough for that!

Some of us, oppressed by our own weakness, may at times have been tempted to think that there are sins which are almost unforgivable. Let us remember the word: "The blood of Jesus Christ his Son cleanses us from every sin." Big sins, small sins, sins which may be very black and sins which appear to be not so black, sins which I think can be forgiven and sins which seem unforgivable, yes, *all* sins, conscious or unconscious, remembered or forgotten, are included in those words: "every sin." "The blood of Jesus his Son cleanses us from every sin," and it does so because in the first place it satisfies God.

Since God, seeing all our sins in the light, can forgive them on the basis of the Blood, what grounds for accusation has Satan? Satan may accuse us before him, but, "If God is for us, who is against us?" (Romans 8:31) God points him to the Blood of his dear Son. It is the sufficient answer against which Satan has no appeal. "Who shall lay anything to the charge of God's elect? It is God that justifieth; who is he that shall condemn? It is Christ Jesus that died, yea rather, that was raised from the dead, who is at

---

[1] 1 John 1:7: Marginal reading of the *New Translation* by J.N. Darby. —*Angus Kinnear* [This was *Darby's New Translation*, 1871. Written by John Nelson Darby (1800–1882), this literal translation offered a more accurate English version of the Bible than the KJV, and was designed especially for study use. The translation is still used today.]

the right hand of God, who also maketh intercession for us" (Romans 8:33–34). Thus God answers his every challenge.

So here again our need is to recognize the absolute sufficiency of the precious Blood. "Christ having come a high priest . . . through his own blood, entered in, once for all, into the holy place, having obtained eternal redemption" (Hebrews 9:11–12). He was Redeemer once. He has been High Priest and Advocate for nearly two thousand years. He stands there in the presence of God, and "he is the propitiation for our sins" (1 John 2:1–2). Note the words of Hebrews 9:14: *"How much more shall the blood of Christ . . . cleanse your conscience."* They underline the sufficiency of his ministry. *It is enough for God.*

What then of our attitude to Satan? This is important, for he accuses us not only before God but in our own conscience also. "You have sinned, and you keep on sinning. You are weak, and God can have nothing more to do with you." This is his argument. And our temptation is to look within and in self-defense to try to find in ourselves, in our feelings or our behavior, some grounds for believing that Satan is wrong. Alternatively, we are tempted to admit our helplessness and, going to the other extreme, to yield to depression and despair. Thus accusation becomes one of the greatest and most effective of Satan's weapons. He points to our sins and seeks to charge us with them before God, and if we accept his accusations we go down immediately.

Now the reason why we so readily accept his accusations is that we are still hoping to have some righteousness of our own. The grounds for our expectation is wrong. Satan has succeeded in making us look in the wrong direction. Thereby he wins his point, rendering us ineffective. But if we have learned to put no confidence in the flesh, we shall not wonder if we sin, for the very nature of the flesh is to sin. Do you understand what I mean? It is because we have not come to appreciate our true nature and to see how helpless we are that we still have some expectation in ourselves, with the result that, when Satan comes along and accuses us, we go down under it.

God is well able to deal with our sins; but he cannot deal with a man under accusation, because such a man is not trusting in the Blood. The Blood speaks in his favor, but he is listening instead to Satan. Christ is our Advocate, but we, the accused, side with the accuser. We have not recognized that we are unworthy of anything but death; that, as we shall shortly see, we are only fit to be crucified anyway. We have not recognized that it is God alone that can answer the accuser, and that in the precious Blood, he has already done so.

Our salvation lies in looking away to the Lord Jesus and in seeing that the Blood of the Lamb has met the whole situation created by our sins and has answered it. That is the sure foundation on which we stand. Never should we try to answer Satan with our good conduct, but always with the Blood. Yes, we are sinful, but, praise God! the Blood cleanses us from every sin. God looks upon the Blood whereby his Son has met the charge, and Satan has no more grounds for attack. Our faith in the precious Blood and our refusal to be moved from that position can alone silence his charges and put him to flight (Romans 8:33–34); and so it will be, right on to the end (Revelation 12:11). Oh, what an emancipation it would be if we saw more of the value of God's eyes of the precious Blood of his dear Son!

Chapter 2

The Cross of Christ

We have seen that Romans 1 to 8 falls into two sections, in the first of which we are shown that the Blood deals with what we have *done*, while in the second we shall see that the Cross[1] deals with what we *are*. We need the Blood for forgiveness; we need also the Cross for deliverance. We have dealt briefly above with the first of these two and we shall move on now to the second; but before we do so we will look for a moment at a few more features of

---

[1] Note: The author uses "the Cross" here and throughout these studies in a special sense. Most readers will be familiar with the current use of the expression "the Cross" to signify, firstly, the entire redemptive work accomplished historically in the death, burial, resurrection and ascension of the Lord Jesus himself (Phil. 2:8–9), and secondly, in a wider sense, the union of believers with him therein through grace (Rom. 6:4; Eph. 2:5–6). Clearly in that use of the term, the operation of "the Blood" in relation to forgiveness of sins (as dealt with in Chapter 1 of this book) is, from God's viewpoint, included (with all that follows in these studies) as a part of the work of the Cross. In this and the following chapters, however, the author is compelled, for lack of an alternative term, to use "the Cross" in a more particular and limited doctrinal sense in order to draw a helpful distinction, namely, that between substitution and identification, as being, from the human angle, two separate aspects of the doctrine of redemption. Thus the name of the whole is of necessity used for one of its parts. The reader should bear this in mind in what follows.—*Angus I. Kinnear, Editor*

this passage which serve to emphasize the striking difference of theme and subject matter between the two halves.

Some Further Distinctions

Two aspects of the resurrection are mentioned in the two sections, in chapters 4 and 6. In Romans 4:25 the resurrection of the Lord Jesus is mentioned in relation to our justification: "Jesus our Lord . . . was delivered up for our trespasses, and was raised for our justification." Here the matter in view is that of our standing before God. But in Romans 6:4 the resurrection is spoken of as imparting to us new life, with a view to a holy walk: "That like as Christ was raised from the dead . . . so we also might walk in newness of life." Here the matter before us is behavior.

Again, peace is spoken of in both sections, in the fifth and eighth chapters. Romans 5 tells of peace with God, which is the effect of justification by faith in his Blood: "Being therefore justified by faith, we have peace with God through our Lord Jesus Christ." (5:1, marg.[2]) This means that, now that I have forgiveness of sins, God will no longer be a cause of dread to me. I who was an enemy to God have been "reconciled . . . through the death of his Son" (5:10). I very soon find, however, that I am going to be a great cause of trouble to myself. There is still unrest within, for within me there is something that draws me to sin. There is peace with God, but there is no peace with myself. There is, in fact, civil war in my own heart. This condition is well depicted in Romans 7, where the flesh and the spirit are seen to be in deadly conflict within me. But from this, the argument leads in chapter 8 to the inward peace of a walk in the Spirit. "The mind of the flesh is death," because it "is enmity against God," "but the mind of the spirit is life and peace" (Romans 8:6–7).

Looking further still, we find that the first half of the section deals, generally speaking, with the question of justification (see, for example, Romans 3:24–26; 4:5, 25), while the second half has as its main topic the corresponding question of sanctification (see Rom. 6:19, 22). When we know the precious truth of justification by faith, we still know only half of

---

[2] Marginal readings (alternate translations) of Bible references are indicated by "marg." after the reference.

the story. We still have only solved the problem of our standing before God. As we go on, God has something more to offer us, namely, the solution of the problem of our conduct—and the development of thought in these chapters serves to emphasize this. In each case the second step follows from the first, and if we know only the first, then we are still leading a sub-normal Christian life. How then can we live a *normal* Christian life? How do we enter upon it? Well, of course, initially we must have forgiveness of sins, we must have justification, we must have peace with God: these are our indispensable foundation. But with that basis truly established through our first act of faith in Christ, it is yet clear from the above that we must move on to something more.

So we see that objectively the Blood deals with *our sins*. The Lord Jesus has borne them on the Cross for us as our Substitute, and has thereby obtained for us forgiveness, justification, and reconciliation. But we must now go a step further in the plan of God to understand how he deals with *the sin principle in us*. The Blood can wash away my sins, but it cannot wash away my "old man." It needs the Cross to crucify me. The Blood deals with the *sins,* but the Cross must deal with the *sinner.*

You will scarcely find the word "sinner" in the first four chapters of Romans. This is because there the sinner himself is not mainly in view, but rather the sins he has committed. The word "sinner" first comes into prominence only in chapter 5, and it is important to notice how the sinner is there introduced. In that chapter, a sinner is said to be a sinner because he is born a sinner; not because he has committed sins. The distinction is important. It is true that often when a Gospel worker wants to convince a man in the street that he is a sinner, he will use the favorite verse Romans 3:23, where it says that "all have sinned"; but this use of the verse is not strictly justified by the Scriptures. Those who so use it are in danger of arguing the wrong way round, for the teaching of Romans is not that we are sinners because we commit sins, but that *we sin because we are sinners.* We are sinners by *constitution* rather than by *action.* As Romans 5:19 expresses it: "Through the one man's disobedience, the many were made (or 'constituted') sinners."

How were we constituted sinners? By Adam's disobedience. We do not become sinners by what we have done, but because of what Adam has done and has become. I speak English, but I am not thereby constituted an

Englishman. I am in fact a Chinese. So chapter 3 draws our attention to what we have done—"all have sinned"—but it is nevertheless not because we have done it that we become sinners.

I once asked a class of children, "Who is a sinner?" and their immediate reply was, "One who sins." Yes, one who sins is a sinner, but the fact that he sins is merely the evidence that he is already a sinner; it is not the cause. One who sins is a sinner, but it is equally true that one who does not sin, if he is of Adam's race, is a sinner too, and in need of redemption. Do you follow me? There are bad sinners and there are good sinners, there are moral sinners and there are corrupt sinners, but they are all alike sinners. We sometimes think that if only we had not done certain things all would be well; but the trouble lies far deeper than in what we do: it lies in what we are. A Chinese may be born in America and be unable to speak Chinese at all, but he is a Chinese for all that, because he was born a Chinese. It is birth that counts. So I am a sinner because I am born in Adam. It is a matter not of my behavior but of my heredity, my parentage. I am not a sinner because I sin, but I sin because I come of the wrong stock. I sin because I am a sinner.

We are apt to think that what we have done is very bad, but that we *ourselves* are not so bad. God is taking pains to show us that we ourselves are wrong, fundamentally wrong. The root trouble is the sinner; he must be dealt with. Our sins are dealt with by the Blood, but we ourselves are dealt with by the Cross. The Blood procures our pardon for what we have *done*; the Cross procures our deliverance from what we *are*.

Man's State By Nature

We come therefore to Romans 5:12–21. In this great passage, grace is brought into contrast with sin and the obedience of Christ is set against the disobedience of Adam. It is placed at the beginning of the second section of Romans (5:12 to 8:39) with which we shall now be particularly concerned, and its argument leads to a conclusion which lies at the very heart of our further meditations. What is that conclusion? It is found in verse 19 already quoted: "For as through the one man's disobedience the many were made sinners, even so through the obedience of the one shall the many be made righteous." Here the Spirit of God is seeking to show us first what we are, and then how it was [that] we came to be what we are.

At the beginning of our Christian life we are concerned with our *doing*, not with our *being*; we are distressed rather by what we have done than by what we are. We think that if only we could rectify certain things we should be good Christians, and we set out therefore to change our actions. But the result is not what we expected. We discover to our dismay that it is something more than just a case of trouble on the outside—that there is in fact more serious trouble on the inside. We try to please the Lord, but find something within that does not *want* to please him. We try to be humble, but there is something in our very being that refuses to be humble. We try to be loving, but inside we feel most unloving. We smile and try to look very gracious, but inwardly we feel decidedly ungracious. The more we try to rectify matters on the outside, the more we realize how deep-seated is the trouble. Then we come to the Lord and say, "Lord, I see it now! Not only what I have *done* is wrong; *I* am wrong."

The conclusion of Romans 5:19 is beginning to dawn upon us. We are sinners. We are members of a race of people who are constitutionally other than what God intended them to be. By the Fall a fundamental change took place in the character of Adam whereby he became a sinner, one constitutionally unable to please God; and the family likeness which we all share is no mere superficial one but extends to our inward character also. We have been "constituted sinners." How did this come about? "By the disobedience of one," says the Apostle. Let me try to illustrate this by a simple analogy.

My name is Nee. It is a fairly common Chinese name. How did I come by it? I did not choose it. I did not go through the list of possible Chinese names and select this one. That my name is Nee is in fact not my doing at all, and, moreover, nothing I can do can alter it. I am a Nee because my father was a Nee, and my father was a Nee because my grandfather was a Nee. If I act like a Nee, I am a Nee, and if I act unlike a Nee, I am still a Nee. If I become President of the Chinese Republic I am a Nee, or if I become a beggar in the street I am still a Nee. Nothing I do or refrain from doing will make me other than a Nee.

We are sinners not because of ourselves but because of Adam. It is not because I individually have sinned that I am a sinner, but because I was in

19

Adam when he sinned. Because by birth I come of Adam, therefore I am a part of him. What is more, I can do nothing to alter this. I cannot by improving my behavior, make myself other than a part of Adam—and so a sinner.

In China I was once talking in this strain and remarked, "We have all sinned in Adam." A man said, "I don't understand," so I sought to explain it in this way.

"All Chinese trace their descent from Huang-ti," I said. "Over four thousand years ago he had a war with Si-iu. His enemy was very strong, but nevertheless Huang-ti overcame and slew him. After this Huang-ti founded the Chinese nation. Four thousand years ago therefore our nation was founded by Huang-ti. Now what would have happened if Huang-ti had not killed his enemy, but had been himself killed instead? Where would you be now?"

"There would be no 'me' at all," he answered.

"Oh, no! Huang-ti can die his death and you can live your life."

"Impossible!" he cried, "If he had died, then I could never have lived, for I have derived my life from him."

Do you see the oneness of human life? Our life comes from Adam. If your great-grandfather had died at the age of three, where would you be? You would have died in him! Your experience is bound up with his. And in just the same way the experience of every one of us is bound up with that of Adam. None can say, "I have not been in Eden" for potentially we all were there when Adam yielded to the serpent's words. So we are all involved in Adam's sin, and by being born "in Adam," we receive from him all that he became as a result of his sin—that is to say, the Adam-nature which is the nature of a sinner. We derive our existence from him, and because his life became a sinful life, a sinful nature, therefore the nature which we derive from him is also sinful. So, as we have said, the trouble is in our heredity, not in our behavior. Unless we can change our parentage there is no deliverance for us.

But it is in this very direction that we shall find the solution of our problem, for that is exactly how God has dealt with it.

As In Adam, So In Christ

In Romans 5:12 to 21 we are not only told something about Adam; we are told also something about the Lord Jesus. "As through the one man's disobedience the many were made sinners, even so through the obedience of the one shall the many be made righteous." In Adam we receive everything that is of Adam; in Christ we receive everything that is of Christ.

The terms "in Adam" and "in Christ" are too little understood by Christians, and, at the risk of repetition, I wish again to emphasize by means of an illustration the hereditary and racial significance of the term "in Christ." This illustration is to be found in the letter to the Hebrews. Do you remember that in the earlier part of that letter the writer is trying to show that Melchizedek is greater than Levi? You recall that the point to be proved is that the priesthood of Christ is greater than the priesthood of Aaron who was of the tribe of Levi. Now in order to prove that, he has first to prove that the priesthood of Melchizedek is greater than the priesthood of Levi, for the simple reason that the priesthood of Christ is "after the order of Melchizedek" (Heb. 7:14–17), while that of Aaron is, of course, after the order of Levi. If the writer can demonstrate to us that, in the eyes of God, Melchizedek is greater than Levi, then he has made his point. That is the issue, and he proves it in a remarkable way.

He tells us in Hebrews chapter 7 that one day Abraham, returning from the battle of the kings (Genesis 14), offered a tithe of his spoils to Melchizedek and received from him a blessing. Inasmuch as Abraham did so, Levi is therefore of less account than Melchizedek. Why? Because the fact that Abraham offered tithes to Melchizedek means that Isaac "in Abraham" offered to Melchizedek. But if that is true, then Jacob also "in Abraham" offered to Melchizedek, which in turn means that Levi "in Abraham" offered to Melchizedek. It is evident that the lesser offers to the greater (Hebrews 7:7). So Levi is less in standing than Melchizedek, and therefore the priesthood of Aaron is inferior to that of the Lord Jesus. Levi at the time of the battle of the kings was not yet even thought of. Yet he was "in the loins of his father" Abraham, and, "so to say, through Abraham," he offered (Hebrews 7:9–10).

Now his is the exact meaning of "in Christ." Abraham, as the head of the family of faith, includes the whole family in himself. When he offered to Melchizedek, the whole family offered in him to Melchizedek. They did not offer separately as individuals, but they were in him, and therefore in making his offering, he included with himself all his seed.

21

So we are presented with a new possibility. In Adam all was lost. Through the disobedience of one man we were all constituted sinners. By him, sin entered, and death through sin—and throughout the race sin has reigned unto death from that day on. But now a ray of light is cast upon the scene. Through the obedience of Another we may be constituted righteous. Where sin abounded, grace did much more abound, and as sin reigned unto death, even so may grace reign through righteousness unto eternal life by Jesus Christ our Lord (Romans 5:19–21). Our despair is in Adam; our hope is in Christ.

The Divine Way of Deliverance

God clearly intends that this consideration should lead to our practical deliverance from sin. Paul makes this quite plain when he opens chapter 6 of his letter with the question: "Shall we continue in sin?" His whole being recoils at the very suggestion. "God forbid!" he exclaims. How could a holy God be satisfied to have unholy, sin-fettered children? And so "how shall we any longer live therein?" (Romans 6:1–2). God has surely therefore made adequate provision that we should be set free from sin's dominion.

But here is our problem. We were born sinners; how then can we cut off our sinful heredity? Seeing that we were born in Adam, how can we get out of Adam? Let me say at once, the Blood cannot take us out of Adam. There is only one way. Since we came in by birth we must go out by death. To do away with our sinfulness we must do away with our life. Bondage to sin came by birth; deliverance from sin comes by death—and it is just this way of escape that God has provided. Death is the secret of emancipation. "We . . . died to sin" (Romans 6:2).

But how can we die? Some of us have tried very hard to get rid of this sinful life, but we have found it most tenacious. What is the way out? It is not by trying to kill ourselves, but by recognizing that *God has dealt with us in Christ.* This is summed up in the apostle's next statement: "All we who were baptized into Christ Jesus were baptized into his death" (Romans 6:3).

But if God has dealt with us "in Christ Jesus," then we have got to *be* in Him for this to become effective, and that now seems just as big a problem. How are we to "get into" Christ? Here again God comes to our help. We have in fact no way of getting in; but, what is more important, we need not try to get in, for we *are* in. What we could not do for ourselves, God has done for us. *He has put us into Christ.* Let me remind you of 1 Corinthians 1:30. I think that is one of the best verses of the whole New Testament: "Ye are in Christ." How? "Of Him (that is, 'of God') are ye in Christ." Praise God! It is not left to us either to devise a way of entry, or to work it out. We need not plan how to get in. God has planned it; and he has not only planned it but he has also performed it. *"Of Him are ye in Christ Jesus."* We are in; therefore we need not try to get in. It is a divine act, and it is accomplished.

Now if this is true, certain things follow. In the illustration from Hebrews 7 which we considered above, we saw that "in Abraham," all Israel—and therefore Levi who was not yet born—offered tithes to Melchizedek. They did not offer separately and individually, but they were in Abraham when he offered, and his offering included all his seed. This, then, is a true figure of ourselves as "in Christ." When the Lord Jesus was on the Cross all of us died—not individually, for we had not yet been born—but, being in him, we died in him. "One died for all, therefore all died" (2 Cor. 5:14). When he was crucified, all of us were crucified there with him.

Many a time when preaching in the villages of China, one has to use very simple illustrations for deep divine truth. I remember once I took up a small book and put a piece of paper into it, and I said to those very simple folk,

> Now look carefully. I take a piece of paper. It has an identity of its own, quite separate from this book. Having no special purpose for it at the moment, I put it into the book. Now I do something with the book. I post it to Shanghai. I do not post the paper, but the paper has been put into the book. Then where is the paper? Can the book go to Shanghai and the paper remain here? Can the paper have a separate destiny from the book? No! Where the book goes the paper goes. If I drop the book in the river the paper goes too, and if I quickly take it out again I recover the paper also. Whatever experience the book goes through the paper goes through with it, for it is still there in the book.

"Of him are ye in Christ Jesus." The Lord God himself has put us in Christ, and in his dealing with Christ, God has dealt with the whole race. Our destiny is bound up with his. What he has gone through we have gone through, for to be "in Christ" is to have been identified with him in both his death and resurrection. He was crucified: then what about us? Must we ask God to crucify us? Never! When Christ was crucified we were crucified; and his crucifixion is past, therefore ours cannot be future. I challenge you to find one text in the New Testament telling us that our crucifixion is in the future. All the references to it are in the Greek *aorist*, which is the "once-for-all" tense, the "eternally past" tense. (See Romans 6:6; Galatians 2:20; 5:24; 6:14). And just as no man could ever commit suicide by crucifixion, for it were a physical impossibility to do so, so also, in spiritual terms, God does not require us to crucify ourselves. We were crucified when Christ was crucified, for God put us there in Him. That we have died in Christ is not merely a doctrinal position: it is an eternal and indisputable fact.

His Death and Resurrection Representative and Inclusive

The Lord Jesus, when he died on the Cross, shed his Blood, thus giving his sinless life to atone for our sin and to satisfy the righteousness and holiness of God. To do so was the prerogative of the Son of God alone. No man could have a share in that. The Scripture has never told us that we shed our blood with Christ. In his atoning work before God, he acted alone; no other could have a part. But the Lord did not die only to shed his Blood: he died that *we* might die. He died as *our* Representative. In his death he included *you and me*.

We often use the terms "substitution" and "identification" to describe these two aspects of the death of Christ. Now, many a time the use of the word "identification" is good. But identification would suggest that the thing begins from our side: that I try to identify myself with the Lord. I agree that the word is true, but it should be used later on. It is better to begin with the fact that the Lord included me in his death. It is the "inclusive" death of the Lord which puts me in a position to identify myself—not that I identify myself in order to be included. It is God's inclusion of me in Christ that matters. It is something God has done. For that reason, those two New Testament words "in Christ" are always very dear to my heart.

The death of the Lord Jesus is inclusive. The resurrection of the Lord Jesus is alike [also] inclusive. We have looked at the first chapter of 1 Corinthians to establish the fact that we are "in Christ Jesus." Now we will go to the end of the same letter to see something more of what this means. In 1 Corinthians 15:45–47, two remarkable names or titles are used of the Lord Jesus. He is spoken of there as "the last Adam" and he is spoken of too as "the second man." Scripture does not refer to him as the second Adam, but as "the last Adam"; nor does it refer to him as the last Man, but as "the second man." The distinction is to be noted, for it enshrines a truth of great value.

As the last Adam, Christ is the sum total of humanity; as the second Man, he is the Head of a new race. So we have here two unions, the one relating to his death and the other to his resurrection. In the first place his union with the race as "the last Adam" began historically at Bethlehem and ended at the cross and the tomb. In it he gathered up into himself all that was in Adam and took it to judgment and death. In the second place our union with him as "the second man" begins in resurrection and ends in eternity—which is to say, it never ends—for, having in his death done away with the first man in whom God's purpose was frustrated, he rose again as Head of a new race of men, in whom that purpose shall be fully realized.

When therefore the Lord Jesus was crucified on the cross, he was crucified as the last Adam. All that was in the first Adam was gathered up and done away in him. We were included there. As the last Adam he wiped out the old race; as the second Man he brings in the new race. It is in his resurrection that he stands forth as the second Man, and there too we are included. "For if we have become united with him by the likeness of his death, we shall be also by the likeness of his resurrection" (Romans 6:5). We died in him as the last Adam; we live in him as the second Man. The Cross is thus the mighty act of God which translates us from Adam to Christ.

CHAPTER 3

The Path of Progress: Knowing

Our old history ends with the Cross; our new history begins with the resurrection. "If any man is in Christ, he is a new creature: the old things are passed away; behold they are become new" (2 Cor 5:17). The Cross terminates the first creation, and out of death there is brought a new creation in Christ, the second Man. If we are "in Adam," all that is in Adam necessarily devolves upon us; it becomes ours involuntarily, for we have to do nothing to get it. There is no need to make up our minds to lose our temper or to commit some other sin; it comes to us freely and despite ourselves. In a similar way, if we are "in Christ," all that is in Christ comes to us by free grace, without effort on our part but on the grounds of simple faith.

But to say that all we need comes to us in Christ by free grace, though true enough, may seem unpractical. How does it work out in life? How does it become real in our experience?

As we study chapters 6, 7, and 8 of Romans, we shall discover that the conditions of living the normal Christian life are fourfold.

27

They are: (a) knowing, (b) reckoning, (c) presenting ourselves to God, and (d) walking in the Spirit—and they are set forth in that order. If we would live that life we shall have to take all four of these steps; not one nor two nor three, but all four. As we study each of them we shall trust the Lord by his Holy Spirit to illumine our understanding; and we shall seek his help now to take the first big step forward.

Our Death with Christ a Historic Fact

Romans 6:1–11 is the passage before us now. In these verses it is made clear that the death of the Lord Jesus is representative and inclusive. In his death we all died. None of us can progress spiritually without seeing this. Just as we cannot have justification if we have not seen him bearing *our sins* on the Cross, so we cannot have sanctification if we have not seen him bearing *us* on the Cross. Not only have our *sins* been laid on him, but we *ourselves* have been put into him.

How did you receive forgiveness? You realized that the Lord Jesus died as your Substitute and bore your sins upon himself, and that his Blood was shed to cleanse away your defilement. When you saw your sins all taken away on the Cross what did you do? Did you say, "Lord Jesus, please come and die for my sins"? No, you did not pray at all; you only thanked the Lord. You did not beseech him to come and die for you, for you realized that he had already done so.

But what is true of your forgiveness is also true of your deliverance. The work is done. There is no need to pray, but only to praise. God has put us all in Christ, so that when Christ was crucified we were crucified also. Thus there is no need to pray: "I am a very wicked person; Lord, please crucify me." That is all wrong. You did not pray about your sins; why pray now about yourself? Your sins were dealt with by his Blood, and you were dealt with by his Cross. It is an accomplished fact. All that is left for you to do is to praise the Lord that when Christ died, you died also; you died in him. Praise him for it, and live in the sight of it. "Then believed they his words: they sang his praise" (Psalm 106:12).

Do you believe in the death of Christ? Of course you do. But the same Scripture that says he died for us, says also that we died with him. Look at it again: "Christ died for us" (Romans 5:8). That is the first statement, and

28

that is clear enough; but is this any less clear? "Our old man was crucified with him" (Romans 6:6). "We died with Christ" (Romans 6:8).

When are we crucified with him? What is the date of our old man's crucifixion? Is it tomorrow? Yesterday? Today? In order to answer this, it may help us if, for a moment, I turn Paul's statement round and say, "Christ was crucified with (i.e. *at the same time as*) our old man." Some of you came here in twos. You traveled to this place together. You might say, "My friend came here with me," but you might just as truly say, "I came here with my friend." Had one of you come three days ago and the other only today you could not possibly say that; but having come together you can make either statement with equal truth, because both are statements of fact. So also in historic fact we can say, reverently but with equal accuracy, "I was crucified when Christ was crucified" or "Christ was crucified when I was crucified," for they are not two historical events, but one. My crucifixion was "with him."[1] Has Christ been crucified? Then can I be otherwise? And if he was crucified nearly two thousand years ago, and I with him, can my crucifixion be said to take place tomorrow? Can his be past, and mine, present or future? Praise the Lord, when he died on the Cross, I died with him. He not only died in my stead, but he bore me with him to the Cross, so that when he died, I also died. And if I believe in the death of the Lord Jesus, then I can believe in my own death just as surely as I believe in his.

Why do you believe that the Lord Jesus died? What are your grounds for that belief? Is it that you *feel* he has died? No, you have never felt it. You believe it because the Word of God tells you so. When the Lord was crucified, two thieves were crucified at the same time. You do not doubt that they were crucified with him, either, because the Scripture says so quite plainly.

You believe in the death of the Lord Jesus and you believe in the death of the thieves with him. Now what about your own death? Your crucifixion is more intimate than theirs. They were crucified at the same time as the Lord but on different crosses, whereas you were crucified on the self-same cross as He, for you were in him when he died. How can you know? You can know for

---

[1] The expression "with him" in Romans 6:6 carries of course a doctrinal as well as historical, or temporal sense. It is only in the historical sense that the statement is reversible. —*Watchman Nee.*

the one sufficient reason that God has said so. It does not depend on your feelings. If you feel that Christ has died, *he has died;* and if you do *not* feel that he has died, *he has died.* If you feel that you have died, you have died; and if you do not feel that you have died, you have nevertheless just as surely died. These are divine facts. That Christ has died is a fact, that the two thieves have died is a fact, and that you have died is a fact also. Let me tell you, *you have died!* You are done with! You are ruled out! The self you loathe is on the Cross in Christ. And "he that is dead is freed from sin" (Romans 6:7, AV[2]). This is the Gospel for Christians.

Our crucifixion can never be made effective by will or by effort, but only by accepting what the Lord Jesus did on the Cross. Our eyes must be opened to see the finished work of Calvary. Some of you, prior to your salvation, may have tried to save yourselves. You read the Bible, prayed, went to church, gave alms. Then one day, your eyes were opened and you saw that a full salvation had already been provided for you on the Cross. You just accepted that, and thanked God, and peace and joy flowed into your heart. And the good news is that sanctification is made possible for you on exactly the same basis as that initial salvation. You are offered *deliverance* from sin as no less a gift of God's grace than was the *forgiveness* of your sins.

For God's way of deliverance is altogether different from man's way. Man's way is to try to suppress sin by seeking to overcome it; God's way is to remove the sinner. Many Christians mourn over their weakness, thinking that if only they were stronger, all would be well. The idea that, *because failure to lead a holy life is due to our impotence, something more is therefore demanded of us,* leads naturally to this false conception of the way of deliverance. If we are preoccupied with the power of sin and with our inability to meet it, then we naturally conclude that to gain the victory over sin we must have more power. "If only I were stronger," we say, "I could overcome my violent outbursts of temper," and so we plead with the Lord to strengthen us that we may exercise more self-control.

But this is altogether a fallacy; this is not Christianity. God's means of delivering us from sin is not by making us stronger and stronger, but by

---

[2] Authorized Version (KJV).

making us weaker and weaker. That is surely rather a peculiar way of victory, you say; but it is the divine way. God sets us free from the dominion of sin, not by strengthening our old man, but by crucifying him; not by helping him to do anything but by removing him from the scene of action.

For years, maybe, you have tried fruitlessly to exercise control over yourself, and perhaps this is still your experience; but when once you see the truth, you will recognize that you are indeed powerless to do anything—but that in setting *you* aside altogether, *God* has done it all. Such a discovery brings human striving and self-effort to an end.

The First Step: "Knowing This . . . "

The normal Christian life must begin with a very definite "knowing," which is not just knowing something about the truth, nor understanding some important doctrine. It is not intellectual knowledge at all, but an opening of the eyes of the heart to see what we have in Christ.

How do you know your sins are forgiven? Is it because your pastor told you so? No, you just *know* it. If I ask you how you know, you simply answer, "I know it!" Such knowledge comes by divine revelation. It comes from the Lord himself. Of course the fact of forgiveness of sins is in the Bible, but for the written Word of God to become a living Word from God to you, he had to give you "a spirit of wisdom and revelation in the knowledge of him" (Eph. 1:17). What you needed was to know *Christ* in that way, and it is always so. So there comes a time, in regard to any new apprehension of Christ, when you know it in your own heart; you "see" it in your spirit. A light has shined into your inner being, and you are wholly persuaded of the fact. What is true of the forgiveness of your sins is no less true of your deliverance from sin. When once the light of God dawns upon your heart, you *see* yourself in Christ. It is not now because someone has told you, and not merely because Romans 6 says so. It is something more even than that. You know it because God has revealed it to you by his Spirit. You may not feel it; you may not understand it; but you *know* it, for you have seen it. Once you have seen yourself in Christ, nothing can shake your assurance of that blessed fact.

If you ask a number of believers who have entered upon the normal Christian life how they came by their experience, some will say "in this way" and some will say "in that." Each stresses his own particular way of entering in, and produces Scripture to support his experience; and unhappily, many Christians are using their special experiences and their special scriptures to fight other Christians. The fact of the matter is that, while Christians may enter into the deeper life by different ways, we need not regard the experiences or doctrines they stress as mutually exclusive, but rather complementary. One thing is certain, that any true experience of value in the sight of God must have been reached by way of a new discovery of the meaning of the person and work of the Lord Jesus. That is a crucial test, and a safe one.

And here in our passage Paul makes everything depend upon such a discovery.

> Knowing this, that our old man was crucified with him, that the body of sin might be done away, that so we should no longer be in bondage to sin (Romans 6:6).

Divine Revelation Essential to Knowledge

So our first step is to seek from God a knowledge that comes by revelation—a revelation, that is to say, not of ourselves but of the finished work of the Lord Jesus Christ on the Cross. When Hudson Taylor, the founder of the China Inland Mission, entered into the normal Christian life, it was thus that he did so. You remember how he tells of his long-standing problem of how to live "in Christ:" how to draw the sap out of the Vine into himself. For he knew that he must have the life of Christ flowing out through him, and yet felt that he had not got it, and he saw clearly enough that his need was to be found *in* Christ. "I knew," he said, writing to his sister from Chinkiang in 1869, "that if only I could abide in Christ, all would be well, but I *could not.*"

The more he tried to get in, the more he found himself slipping out, so to speak, until one day light dawned, revelation came, and he saw.

> Here, I feel, is the secret: not asking how I am to get sap *out* of the Vine into myself, but remembering that Jesus *is* the Vine—the root, stem, branches, twigs, leaves, flowers, fruit, all indeed.

32

Then, quoting a friend's words that had helped him, he continues:

> I have not got to *make* myself a branch. The Lord Jesus tells me I *am* a branch. I am *part of him*—and I have just to believe it and act upon it. I have seen it long enough in the Bible, but I believe it now as a living reality.

It was as though something which had indeed been true all the time had now suddenly become true in a new way to him personally, and he writes to his sister again:

> I do not know how far I may be able to make myself intelligible about it, for there is nothing new or strange or wonderful—and yet, all is new! In a word, "whereas once I was blind, now I see" . . . . I am dead and buried with Christ—aye, and risen too and ascended . . . . God reckons me so, and tells me to reckon myself so. He knows best . . . . Oh, the joy of seeing this truth—I do pray that the eyes of your understanding may be enlightened, that you may know and enjoy the riches freely given us in Christ. [3]

Oh, it is a great thing to see that we are in Christ! Think of the bewilderment of trying to get into a room in which you already are! Think of the absurdity of asking to be put in! If we recognize the fact that we *are* in, we make no effort to enter. If we had more revelation, we should have fewer prayers and more praises. Much of our praying for ourselves is just because we are blind to what God has done.

I remember one day in Shanghai, I was talking with a brother who was very exercised concerning his spiritual state.

He said, "So many are living beautiful, saintly lives. I am ashamed of myself. I call myself a Christian and yet when I compare myself with others I feel I am not one at all. I want to know this crucified life, this resurrection life, but I do not know it and see no way of getting there."

Another brother was with us, and the two of us had been talking for two hours or so, trying to get the man to see that he could not have anything apart from Christ, but without success. Said our friend, "The best thing a man can do is to pray."

"But if God has already given you everything, what do you need to pray for?" we asked.

---

[3] The quotations are from *Hudson Taylor and the China Inland Mission* [1919] by Dr. and Mrs. Howard Taylor, Chapter 12, "The Exchanged Life." The whole passage should be read.—*Angus Kinnear*

"He hasn't," the man replied, "for I am still losing my temper, still failing constantly; so I must pray more."

"Well," we said, "do you get what you pray for?"

"I am sorry to say that I do not get anything," he replied.

We tried to point out that, just as he had done nothing for his justification, so he need do nothing for his sanctification.

Just then a third brother, much used of the Lord, came in and joined us. There was a thermos flask on the table, and this brother picked it up and said, "What is this?"

"A thermos flask."

"Well, you just imagine for a moment that this thermos flask can pray, and that it starts praying something like this: 'Lord, I want very much to be a thermos flask. Wilt thou make me to be a thermos flask? Lord, give me grace to become a thermos flask. Do please make me one!' What will you say?"

"I do not think even a thermos flask would be so silly," our friend replied. "It would be nonsense to pray like that; it *is* a thermos flask!"

Then my brother said, "You are doing the same thing. God in times past has already included you in Christ. When he died, you died; when he lived, you lived. Now today you cannot say, 'I want to die; I want to be crucified; I want to have resurrection life.' The Lord simply looks at you and says, 'You *are* dead! You *have* new life!' All your praying is just as absurd as that of the thermos flask. You do not need to pray to the Lord for anything; you merely need your eyes opened to see that he has done it all."

That is the point. We need not work to die, we need not wait to die; we *are* dead. We only need to recognize what the Lord has already done and to praise him for it. Light dawned for that man.

With tears in his eyes he said, "Lord, I praise thee that thou hast already included me in Christ. All that is his, is mine!" Revelation had come, and faith had something to lay hold of; and if you could have met that brother later on, what a change you would have found!

The Cross Goes to the Root of Our Problem

Let me remind you again of the fundamental nature of that which the Lord has done on the Cross. I feel I cannot press this point too much, for we *must* see it. Suppose, for the sake of illustration, that the government of your country should wish to deal drastically with the question of strong drink, and should decide that the whole country was to go "dry," how could the decision be carried into effect? How could we help? If we were to search every shop and house throughout the land and smash all the bottles of wine or beer or brandy we came across, would that meet the case? Surely not. We might thereby rid the land of every drop of alcoholic liquor it contains, but behind those bottles of strong drink are the factories that produce them, and if we only deal with the bottles and leave the factories untouched, production will still continue and there is no permanent solution of the problem. The drink-producing factories, the breweries and distilleries throughout the land, must be closed down if the drink question is ever to be effectively and permanently settled.

We are the factory; our actions are the products. The Blood of the Lord Jesus dealt with the question of the products, namely, our sins. So the question of what we have done is settled, but would God have stopped there? What about the question of what we are? Our sins were produced by us. They have been dealt with, but how are *we* going to be dealt with? Do you believe the Lord would cleanse away all our sins and then leave us to get rid of the sin-producing factory? Do you believe that, having put away the goods produced, he would leave us to deal by ourselves with the source of production?

To ask this question is but to answer it. Of course he has not done half the work and left the other half undone. No, he has done away with the goods and also made a clean sweep of the factory that produces the goods.

The finished work of Christ really has gone to the root of our problem and dealt with it. There are no half measures with God. He has made full provision for sin's rule to be utterly broken.

"Knowing this," says Paul, "that our old man was crucified with him, that the body of sin might be done away, that so we should no longer be in bondage to sin" (Rom. 6:6). *"Knowing this!"* Yes, but *do* you know it? "Or are ye ignorant?" (Rom. 6:3). May the Lord graciously open our eyes.

Chapter 4

The Path of Progress: Reckoning

We now come to a matter on which there has been some confusion of thought among the Lord's children. It concerns what follows this knowledge. Note again first of all the wording of Romans 6:6: "Knowing this, that our old man was crucified with him." The tense of the verb is most precious, for it puts the event right back there in the past. It is final, once-for-all. The thing has been done, and cannot be undone. Our old man has been crucified once and forever, and he can never be uncrucified. This is what we need to know.

Then, when we know this, what follows? Look again at our passage. The next command is in verse 11: "Even so, reckon ye also yourselves to be dead unto sin." This, clearly, is the natural sequel to verse 6. Read them together: "*Knowing* that our old man was crucified, . . . reckon ye yourselves to be dead." That is the order. When we know that our old man has been crucified with Christ, then the next step is to reckon it so.

Unfortunately, in presenting the truth of our union with Christ, the emphasis has too often been placed upon this second matter of reckoning ourselves to be dead, as though that were the starting point, whereas it should rather be upon *knowing* ourselves to be dead. God's Word makes it clear that "knowing" is to precede "reckoning." "Knowing this . . . reckon." The sequence is most important. Our reckoning must be based on [our] knowledge of divinely revealed fact, for otherwise faith has no foundation on which to rest. When we *know,* then we *reckon* spontaneously.

So in teaching this matter, we should not over-emphasize reckoning. People are always trying to reckon without knowing. They have not first had a Spirit-given revelation of the fact; yet they try to reckon, and soon they get into all sorts of difficulties. When temptation comes, they begin to reckon furiously: "I am dead; I am dead; I am dead!" but in the very act of reckoning, they lose their temper. Then they say, "It doesn't work. Romans 6:11 is no good." And we have to admit that verse 11 *is* no good without verse 6. So it comes to this: that unless we *know* for a fact that we are dead with Christ, the more we *reckon,* the more intense will the struggle become, and the issue [result] will be sure defeat.

For years after my conversion I had been taught to reckon. I reckoned from 1920 until 1927. The more I reckoned that I was dead to sin, the more alive I clearly was. I simply could not believe myself dead, and I could not produce the death. Whenever I sought help from others, I was told to read Romans 6:11, and the more I read Romans 6:11 and tried to reckon, the further away death was: I could not get at it. I fully appreciated the teaching that I must reckon, but I could not make out why nothing resulted from it. I have to confess that for months I was troubled. I said to the Lord,

> If this is not clear, if I cannot be brought to see this which is so very fundamental, I will cease to do anything. I will not preach any more; I will not go out to serve thee any more; I want first of all to get thoroughly clear here.

For months I was seeking, and at times I fasted, but nothing came through.

I remember one morning—that morning was a real morning, and one I can never forget—I was upstairs sitting at my desk reading the Word and praying, and I said, "Lord, open my eyes!" And then in a flash I saw it. I saw my oneness with Christ. I saw that I was in him, and that when he died, I died. I saw that the question of my death was a matter of the past, and not of the future, and that I was just as truly dead as he was, because I was in him when he died. The whole thing had dawned upon me. I was carried away with such joy at this great discovery that I jumped from my chair and cried, "Praise the Lord, I am dead!" I ran downstairs and met one of the brothers helping in the kitchen and I laid hold of him. "Brother," I said, "do you know that I have died?" I must admit he looked puzzled. "What do you mean?" he said, so I went on: "Do you not know that Christ has died? Do you not know that I died with him? Do you not know that my death is no less truly a fact than his?" Oh, it was so real to me! I longed to go through the streets of Shanghai shouting the news of my discovery. From that day to this I have never for one moment doubted the finality of that word: "I have been crucified with Christ."

I do not mean to say that we need not work that out. Yes, there is an outworking of the death, which we are going to see presently, but this, first of all, its basis. I have been crucified: it has been done.

What, then, is the secret of reckoning? To put it in one word, it is *revelation*. We need revelation from God himself (Matt. 16:17; Eph. 1:17–18). We need to have our eyes opened to the fact of our union with Christ, and that is something more than knowing it as a doctrine. Such revelation is no vague, indefinite thing. Most of us can remember the day when we saw clearly that Christ died for us, and we ought to be equally clear as to the time when we saw that we died with Christ. It should be nothing hazy, but very definite, for it is with this as basis that we shall go on. It is not that I reckon myself to be dead, and therefore I *will* be dead. It is that, because I *am* dead—because I see now what God has done with me in Christ—*therefore* I reckon myself to be dead. That is the right kind of reckoning. It is not reckoning *toward* death, but *from* death.

The Second Step: "Even So Reckon . . . "

What does reckoning mean? "Reckoning" in Greek means doing accounts: book-keeping. Accounting is the only thing in the world we human beings can do correctly. An artist paints a landscape. Can he do it with perfect accuracy? Can the historian vouch for the absolute accuracy of any record, or the map-maker for the perfect correctness of any map? They can make, at best, fair approximations. Even in everyday speech, when we try to tell some incident with the best intention to be honest and truthful, we cannot speak with complete accuracy. It is mostly a case of exaggeration or understatement, of one word too much or too little. What then can a man do that is utterly reliable? Arithmetic! There is no scope for error there. One chair plus one chair equals two chairs. That is true in London and it is true in Cape Town. If you travel west to New York or east to Singapore it is still the same. All the world over and for all time, one plus one equals two. One plus one is two in Heaven and Earth and Hell.

Why does God say we are to reckon ourselves dead? Because we *are* dead. Let us keep to the analogy of accounting. Suppose I have fifteen shillings in my pocket: what do I enter in my account-book? Can I enter fourteen shillings and sixpence or fifteen shillings and sixpence? No, I must enter in my account-book that which is, in fact, in my pocket. Accounting is the reckoning of facts, not fancies. Even so, it is because I am really dead that God tells me to account it so. God could not ask me to put down in my account-book what was not true. He could not ask me to reckon that I am dead if I am still alive. For such mental gymnastics the word "reckoning" would be inappropriate; we might rather speak of "mis-reckoning"!

Reckoning is not a form of make-believe. It does not mean that, having found that I have only twelve shillings in my pocket, I hope that, by entering fifteen shillings incorrectly in my account-book, such "reckoning" will somehow remedy the deficiency. It won't. If I have only twelve shillings, yet try to reckon to myself: "I have fifteen shillings; I have fifteen shillings; I have fifteen shillings," do you think that the mental effort involved will in any way affect the sum that is in my pocket? Not a bit of it! Reckoning will not make twelve shillings into fifteen shillings, nor will it make what is untrue true. But if, on the other hand, it is a fact that I have fifteen shillings in my pocket, then with great ease and assurance I can enter fifteen shillings in my account-book. God tells us to reckon ourselves dead, not that by the process of reckoning we may become dead, but because we are dead. He never told us to reckon what was not a *fact*.

Having said, then, that revelation leads spontaneously to reckoning, we must not lose sight of the fact that we are presented with a command: "Reckon ye . . . ." There is a definite attitude to be taken. God asks us to do the account; to put down "I have died," and then to abide by it. Why? Because it is a fact. When the Lord Jesus was on the cross, I was there in him.

Therefore I reckon it to be true. I reckon and declare that I have died in him. Paul said, "Reckon ye also yourselves to be dead unto sin, but alive unto God." How is this possible? "In Christ Jesus." Never forget that it is always and only true *in Christ*. If you look at yourself, you will think death is not there, but it is a question of faith, not in yourself, but in him. You look to the Lord, and know what he has done. "Lord, I believe *in thee*. I reckon upon the fact *in thee*." Stand there all the day.

The Reckoning of Faith

The first four and a half chapters of Romans speak of faith, and faith, and faith. We are justified by faith in him (Rom. 3:28; 5:1). Righteousness, the forgiveness of our sins, and peace with God are all ours by faith, and without faith in the finished work of Jesus Christ none can possess them. But in the second section of Romans we do not find the same repeated mention of faith, and it might at first appear that the emphasis is therefore different. It is not really so, however, for where the words "faith" and "believe" drop out the work "reckon" takes their place. Reckoning and faith are here practically the same thing.

What is faith? Faith is my acceptance of God's fact. It always has its foundations in the past. What relates to the future is hope rather than faith, although faith often has its object or goal in the future, as in Hebrews 11. Perhaps for this reason, the word chosen here is "reckon." It is a word that relates *only* to the past—to what we look back to as settled, and not forward to as yet to be. This is the kind of faith described in Mark 11:24: "All things whatsoever ye pray and ask for, believe that ye have received them, and ye shall have them." The statement there is that, if you believe that you already *have received* your requests (that is, of course, in Christ), then "you shall have them." To believe that you *may* get something, or that you *can* get it, or even that you *will* get it, is not faith in the sense meant here. This is faith—to believe that you have already got it. Only that which relates to the past is faith in this sense. Those who say "God can" or "God may" or "God must" or "God will" do not necessarily believe at all. Faith always says, "God *has* done it."

When, therefore, do I have faith in regard to my crucifixion? Not when I say God can, or will, or must, crucify me, but when with joy I say, "Praise God, in Christ *I am crucified!*"

41

In Romans 3 we see the Lord Jesus bearing our sins and dying as our Substitute, that we might be forgiven. In Romans 6 we see ourselves included in the death whereby he secured our deliverance. When the first fact was revealed to us, we believed on him for our justification. God tells us to reckon upon the second fact for our deliverance. So that, for practical purposes, "reckoning" in the second section of Romans takes the place of "faith" in the first section. The emphasis is not different. The normal Christian life is lived progressively, as it is entered initially, by faith in divine fact: in Christ and his Cross.

Temptation and Failure, the Challenge to Faith

For us, then, the two greatest facts in history are these: that all our sins are dealt with by the Blood, and that we ourselves are dealt with by the Cross. But what now of the matter of temptation? What is to be our attitude when, after we have seen and believed these facts, we discover the old desires rising up again? Worse still, what if we fall once more into known sin? What if we lose our temper, or worse? Is the whole position set forth above proved thereby to be false?

Now remember, one of the Devil's main objects is always to make us doubt the divine facts. (Compare Gen. 3:4.) After we have seen, by revelation of the Spirit of God, that we are indeed dead with Christ, and have reckoned it so, he will come and say: "There is something moving inside. What about it? Can you call this death?" When that happens, what will be our answer? The crucial test is just here. Are we going to believe the tangible facts of the natural realm which are clearly before our eyes, or the intangible facts of the spiritual realm, which are neither seen nor scientifically proved?

Now we must be careful. It is important for us to recall again what are facts stated in God's Word for faith to lay hold of, and what are not. How does God state that deliverance is effected? Well, in the first place, we are not told that sin as a principle in us is rooted out or removed. To reckon on that will be to miscalculate altogether and find ourselves in the false position of the man we considered earlier, who tried to put down the twelve shillings in his pocket as fifteen shillings in his account-book. No, sin is not eradicated. It is very much there, and, given the opportunity, will overpower us and cause us to commit sins again, whether consciously or unconsciously. That is why we shall always need to know the operation of the precious Blood.

But whereas we know that, in dealing with sins committed, God's method is direct, to blot them out of remembrance by means of the Blood, when we come to the principle of sin and the matter of deliverance from its power, we find instead that God deals with this indirectly. He does not remove the sin, but the sinner. Our old man was crucified with him, and because of this the body, which before had been a vehicle of sin, is unemployed (Romans 6:6).[1] Sin, the old master, is still about, but the slave who served him has been put to death and so is out of reach, and his members are unemployed. The gambler's hand is unemployed, the swearer's tongue is unemployed, and these members are now available to be used instead "as instruments of righteousness unto God" (Romans 6:13).

Thus we can say that "deliverance from sin" is a more scriptural idea than "victory over sin." The expressions "freed from sin" and "dead unto sin" in Romans 6:7 and 11 imply deliverance from a power that is still very present and very real—not from something that no longer exists. Sin is still there, but we are knowing deliverance from its power in increasing measure day by day.

This deliverance is so real that John can boldly write: "Whosoever is begotten of God doeth no sin . . . he cannot sin" (1 John 3:9), which is, however, a statement that, wrongly understood, may easily mislead us. By it John is not telling us that sin is now no longer in our history and that we shall not again commit sin. He is saying that to sin is not in the nature of that which is born of God. The life of Christ has been planted in us by new birth and its nature is not to commit sin. But there is a great difference between the nature and the history of a thing, and there is a great difference between the nature of the life within us and *our* history. To illustrate this (though the illustration is an inadequate one) we might say that wood "cannot" sink, for it is not its nature to do so; but of course in history it will do so if a hand holds it under water. The history is a fact, just as sins in our history are historic facts; but the nature is a fact also, and so is the new nature that we have received in Christ. What is "in

---

[1] The verb *katargeo* translated "destroyed" in Romans 6:6 (AV) does not mean "annihilated," but "put out of operation," "made ineffective." It is from the Greek root *argos*, "inactive," "not working," "unprofitable," which is the word translated "idle" in Matthew 20:3, 6 of the unemployed laborers in the market place.—*Angus Kinnear*

Christ" cannot sin; what is in Adam can sin, and will do so whenever Satan is given a chance to exert his power.

So it is a question of our choice of which facts we will count upon and live by: the tangible facts of daily experience or the mightier fact that we are now "in Christ." The power of his resurrection is on our side, and the whole might of God is at work in our salvation (Rom. 1:16), but the matter still rests upon our making real in history what is true in divine fact.

"Now faith is the assurance of things hoped for, the proving of things not seen" (Heb. 11:1), and "the things which are not seen are eternal" (2 Cor. 4:18). I think we all know that Hebrews 11:1 is the only definition of faith in the New Testament, or indeed in the Scriptures. It is important that we should really understand that definition. You are familiar with the common English translation of these words, describing faith as "the substance of things hoped for" (AV). However, the word in the Greek has in it the sense of an action, and not just of some thing, a "substance"—and I confess I have personally spent a number of years trying to find a correct word to translate this. But the New Translation of J.N. Darby[2] is especially good in regard to this word: "Faith is the *substantiating* of things hoped for." That is much better. It implies the making of them real in experience.

How do we "substantiate" something? We are doing so every day. We cannot live in the world without doing so. Do you know the difference between substance and "substantiating"? A substance is an object, something before me. "Substantiating" means that I have a certain power or faculty that makes that substance to be real to me. Let us take a simple illustration. By means of our senses we can take things of the world of nature and transfer them into our consciousness so that we can appreciate them. Sight and hearing, for example, are two of my faculties which substantiate to me the world of light and sound. We have colors: red, yellow, green, blue, violet; and these colors are real things. But if I shut my eyes, then to me the color is no longer real; it is simply nothing—*to me*. With my faculty of sight, however, I possess the power to "substantiate," and by that power, yellow becomes yellow *to me*. It is not only that the color is there, but I have the power to "substantiate" it. I

---

[2] *See note, page 11.*

have the power to make that color true to me and to give it reality in my consciousness. That is the meaning of "substantiating."

If I am blind I cannot distinguish color, or if I lack the faculty of hearing I cannot enjoy music. Yet music and color are in fact *real* things, and their reality is unaffected by whether or not I am able to appreciate them. Now we are considering here the things which, though they are not seen, are eternal and therefore real. Of course we cannot substantiate divine things with any of our natural senses; but there is one faculty which can substantiate the "things hoped for," the things of Christ, and that is faith. Faith makes the *real* things to become real *in my experience.* Faith "substantiates" *to me* the things of Christ. Hundreds of thousands of people are reading Romans 6:6: "Our old man was crucified with him." To faith it is true; to doubt, or to mere mental assent apart from spiritual illumination, it is not true.

Let us remember again that we are dealing here not with *promises* but with *facts.* The promises of God are revealed to us by his Spirit that we may lay hold of then; but facts are facts and they remain facts whether we believe them or not. If we do not believe the facts of the Cross they still remain as real as ever, but they are valueless to us. It does not need faith to make these things real in themselves, but faith can "substantiate" them and make them real in our experience.

Whatever contradicts the truth of God's Word, we are to regard as the Devil's lie, not because it may not be in itself a very real fact to our senses, but because God has stated a greater fact before which the other must eventually yield. I once had an experience which (though not applicable in detail to the present matter) illustrates this principle. Some years ago I was ill. For six nights I had high fever and could find no sleep. Then at length God gave me from the Scripture a personal word of healing, and because of this I expected all symptoms of sickness to vanish at once. Instead of that, not a wink of sleep could I get, and I was not only sleepless but more restless than ever. My temperature rose higher, my pulse beat faster and my head ached more severely than before. The enemy asked, "Where is God's promise? Where is your faith? What about all your prayers?" So I was tempted to thrash the whole matter out in prayer again, but was rebuked, and this Scripture came to mind: "Thy word is truth"

(John 17:17). If God's Word is truth, I thought, then what are these symptoms? They must all be lies! So I declared to the enemy,

> This sleeplessness is a lie, this headache is a lie, this fever is a lie, this high pulse is a lie. In view of what God has said to me, all these symptoms of sickness are just your lies, and God's Word to me is truth.

In five minutes I was asleep, and I awoke the following morning perfectly well.

Now of course in a particular personal matter such as the above, it might be quite possible for me to deceive myself as to what God had said, but of the fact of the Cross there can never be any such question. We *must* believe God, no matter how convincing Satan's arguments appear.

A skillful liar lies not only in word but in gesture and deed; he can as easily pass a bad coin as tell an untruth. The Devil is a skillful liar, and we cannot expect him to stop at words in his lying. He will resort to lying signs and feelings and experiences in his attempts to shake us from our faith in God's Word. Let me make it clear that I do not deny the reality of the "flesh." Indeed we shall have a good deal more to say about this further on in our study. But I am speaking here of our being moved from a revealed position in Christ. As soon as we have accepted our death with Christ as a fact, Satan will do his best to demonstrate convincingly by the evidence of our day-to-day experience that we are not dead at all, but very much alive. So we must choose. Will we believe Satan's lie or God's truth? Are we going to be governed by appearances or by what God says?

I am Mr. Nee. I know that I am Mr. Nee. It is a fact upon which I can confidently count. It is of course possible that I might lose my memory and forget that I am Mr. Nee, or I might dream that I am some other person. But whether I feel like it or not, when I am sleeping I am Mr. Nee, and when I am awake I am Mr. Nee; when I remember it I am Mr. Nee, and when I forget it I am still Mr. Nee.

Now of course, were I to pretend to be someone else, things would be much more difficult. If I were to try and pose as Miss K., I should have to keep saying to myself all the time, "You are Miss K.; now be sure to remember that you are Miss K.," and despite much reckoning the likelihood would be that when I was off my guard and someone called, "Mr. Nee!" I should be caught out and should answer to my own name. Fact would triumph over fiction, and all my reckoning would break down at that crucial moment. But I *am* Mr. Nee, and therefore I have no difficulty whatever in reckoning myself to be Mr. Nee. It is a fact which nothing I experience—or fail to experience—can alter.

So also, whether I feel it or not, I am dead with Christ. How can I be sure? Because Christ has died; and since "one died for all, therefore all died" (2 Cor. 5:14). Whether my experience proves it or seems to disprove it, the fact remains unchanged. While I stand upon that fact, Satan cannot prevail against me. Remember that his attack is always upon our assurance. If he can get us to doubt God's Word, then his object is secured and he has us in his power; but if we rest unshaken in the assurance of God's stated fact, assured that he cannot do injustice to his work or his Word, then it does not matter what tactics Satan adopts, we can well afford to laugh at him. If anyone should try to persuade me that I am not Mr. Nee, I could well afford to do the same.

"We walk by faith, not by appearance" (2 Cor. 5:7, marg.). You probably know the illustration of Fact, Faith and Experience, [as they were] walking along the top of a wall. Fact walked steadily on, turning neither to right nor left and never looking behind. Faith followed and all went well so long as he kept his eyes focused upon Fact; but as soon as he became concerned about Experience and turned to see how he was getting on, he lost his balance and tumbled off the wall, and poor old Experience fell down after him.

All temptation is primarily to look within; to take our eyes off the Lord and to take account of appearances. Faith is always meeting a mountain, a mountain of evidence that seems to contradict God's Word, a mountain of apparent contradiction in the realm of tangible fact—of failures in deed, as well as in the realm of feeling and suggestion—and either faith or the mountain has to go. They cannot both stand. But, the trouble is that many a time the mountain stays and faith goes. That must not be. If we resort to our senses to discover the truth, we shall find Satan's lies are often enough true to our experience; but if we refuse to accept as binding anything that contradicts God's Word and maintain an attitude of faith in him alone, we shall find instead that Satan's lies begin to dissolve and that *our experience is coming progressively to tally with that Word.*

It is our occupation with Christ that has this result, for it means that he becomes progressively real to us on concrete issues. In a given situation we see him as *real* righteousness, *real* holiness, *real* resurrection life—*for us*. What we see in him objectively now operates in us subjectively—but *really*—to manifest him in us, in that situation. That is the mark of maturity. That is what Paul means by his words to the Galatians: "I am again in travail until Christ be formed in you" (4:19). Faith is "substantiating" God's facts; and faith is always the "substantiating" of eternal fact—of something eternally true.

Abiding in Him

Now although we have already spent long on this matter, there is a further thing that may help to make it clearer to us. The Scriptures declare that we are "dead indeed," but nowhere do they say that we are dead *in ourselves*. We shall look in vain to find death within; that is just the place where it is not to be found. We are dead not in ourselves but *in Christ*. We were crucified with him because we were in him.

We are familiar with the words of the Lord Jesus, "Abide in me, and I in you" (John 15:4). Let us consider them for a moment. First, they remind us once again that we have never to struggle to get into Christ. We are not told to *get* there, for we *are* there; but we are told to *stay* there, where we have been placed. It was God's own act that put us in Christ, and we are to *abide* in him.

But further, this verse lays down for us a divine principle, which is that God has done the work in Christ, and not in us as individuals. The all-inclusive death and the all-inclusive resurrection of God's Son were accomplished fully and finally apart from us in the first place. It is the history of *Christ* which is to become the experience of the Christian, and we have no spiritual experience apart from him. The Scriptures tell us that we were crucified "with him," that we were quickened, raised, and set by God in the heavenlies "in him," and that we are complete "in him" (Rom. 6:6; Eph. 2:5–6; Col. 2:10). It is not just something that is still to be effected in us (though it *is* that, of course). It is something that has already been effected, *in association with him*.

In the Scriptures we find that no Christian experience exists *as such*. What God has done in his gracious purpose is to include us in Christ. In dealing with Christ, God has dealt with the Christian; in dealing with the Head, he has dealt with all the members. It is altogether wrong for us to think that we can experience anything of the spiritual life in ourselves merely, and apart from him. God does not intend that we should acquire something exclusively personal in our experience, and he is not willing to effect anything like that for you and me. All the spiritual experience of the Christian *is already true in Christ*. It has already been experienced by Christ. What we call "our" experience is only our entering into his history and his experience.

It would be odd if one branch of a vine tried to bear grapes with a reddish skin, and another branch tried to bear grapes with a green skin, and yet another branch, grapes with a very dark purple skin, each branch trying to produce something of its own without reference to the vine. It is impossible, unthinkable. The character of the branches is determined by the vine. Yet certain Christians are seeking experiences *as experiences.* They think of crucifixion as something, of resurrections as something, of ascension as something, and they never stop to think that the whole is related to a Person. No, only as the Lord opens our eyes to see the Person, do we have any true experience. Every true spiritual experience means that we have discovered a certain fact in Christ and have entered into that; anything that is not from him in this way is an experience that is going to evaporate very soon. "I have discovered *that* in Christ; then, praise the Lord, it is mine! I possess it, Lord, because it is in thee." Oh it is a great thing to know the facts of Christ as the foundation for our experience.

So God's basic principle in leading us on experimentally is not to give us something. It is not to bring us through something, and as a result to put something into us which we can call "*our* experience." It is not that God effects something within *us* so that we can say, "I died with Christ last March" or "I was raised from the dead on January 1st, 1937," or even, "Last Wednesday I asked for a definite experience and I have got it." No, that is not the way. I do not seek experiences *in themselves* as in this present year of grace. Where spiritual history is concerned, time must not be allowed to dominate my thinking.

Then, some will say, what about the crises so many of us have passed through? True, some of us have passed through real crises in our lives. For instance, George Müller[3] could say, bowing himself down to the ground, "There was a day when George Müller died." How about that? Well, I am not questioning the reality of the spiritual experiences we go through nor the importance of crises to which God brings us in our walk with him; indeed, I have already stressed the need for us to be quite as definite ourselves about such crises in our own lives. But the point is that God does not give individuals, individual experiences. All that they have, is only an entering into what God has already done. It is the "realizing" in *time* of *eternal* things. The history of Christ becomes our experience and our spiritual history; we do not have a separate history from his. The entire work with respect to us is not done in us here but in Christ. He does no separate work in individuals apart from what he has done there. Even eternal life is not given to us as individuals: the life is in the Son, and "he that hath the Son hath the life." God has done all in his Son, and he has included us in him; we are incorporated into Christ.

Now the point of all this is that there is a very real practical value in the stand of faith that says, "God has put me in Christ, and therefore all that is true of him is true of me. I will abide in him." Satan is always trying to get us out, to keep us out, to convince us that we are out; and by temptations, failures, suffering, trial, to make us feel acutely that we are outside of Christ. Our first thought is that, if we were in Christ, we should not be in this state, and therefore, judging by the feelings we now have, we must be out of him; and so we begin to pray, "Lord, put me into Christ." No! God's injunction is to "abide" in Christ, and that is the way of deliverance. But how is it so? Because it opens the way for God to take a hand in our lives and to work the thing out in us. It makes room for the operation of his superior power—the power of resurrection (Rom. 6:4, 9–10)—so that the facts of Christ do progressively become the facts of our daily experience, and where before "sin reigned" (Rom. 5:21) we make now the joyful discovery that we are truly "no longer . . . in bondage to sin" (Rom. 6:6).

As we stand steadfastly on the ground of what Christ is, we find that all that is true of him is becoming experimentally true in us. If instead we come on to the ground of what we are in ourselves, we will find that all that is true of the old nature, remains true of us. If we get *there* in faith we have everything; if we return back *here* we find nothing. So often we go to the wrong place to find the death of self. It is in Christ. We have only to look within to find we are very much alive to sin; but when we look over there to the Lord, God sees to it that death works here, but that "newness of life" is ours also. We are "alive unto God" (Rom. 6:4, 11).

"Abide in me, and I in you." This is a double sentence: a command coupled with a promise. That is to say, there is an objective and a subjective side to God's working, and the subjective side depends upon the objective; the "I in you" is the outcome of our abiding in him. We need to guard against being over-anxious about the subjective side of things, and so becoming turned in upon ourselves. We need to dwell upon the objective—"abide in me"—and to let God take care of the subjective. And this he has undertaken to do.

I have illustrated this from the electric light. You are in a room and it is growing dark. You would like to have the light on in order to read. There is a reading-lamp on the table beside you. What do you do? Do you watch it intently to see if the light will come on? Do you take a cloth and polish the bulb? No, you get up and cross over to the other side of the room where the switch is on the wall and you turn the current on. You turn your attention to the source of power and when you have taken the necessary action *there* the light comes on *here.*

So in our walk with the Lord, our attention must be fixed on Christ. "Abide in me, and I in you" is the divine order. Faith in the objective facts make those facts true subjectively. As the apostle Paul puts it, "We all . . . beholding . . . the glory of the Lord, are transformed into the same image" (2 Cor. 3:18, marg.). The same principle holds good in the matter of fruitfulness of life: "He that abideth in me, and I in him, the same beareth much fruit" (John 15:5). We do not try to produce fruit or concentrate upon the fruit produced. Our business is to look away to him. As we do so, he undertakes to fulfill his Word in us.

How do we abide? "Of God are ye in Christ Jesus." It was the work of God to put you there, and he has done it. Now *stay* there! Do not be moved back onto your own ground. Never look at yourself as though you were not in Christ. Look at Christ and see yourself in him. *Abide in him.* Rest in the fact that God has put you in his Son, and live in the expectation that he will complete his work in you. It is for him to make good the glorious promise that "sin shall not have dominion over you" (Rom. 6:14).

CHAPTER 5

The Divide of the Cross

The kingdom of this world is not the kingdom of God. God had in his heart a world-system—a universe of his creating—which should be headed up in Christ his Son (Col. 1:16–17). But Satan, working through man's flesh, has set up instead a rival system known in Scripture as "this world"—a system in which we are involved, and which he himself dominates. He has in fact become "the prince of this world" (John 12:31).

Two Creations

Thus, in Satan's hand, the first creation has become the old creation, and God's primary concern is now no longer with that, but with a second and new creation. He is bringing in a new creation, a new kingdom and a new world, and nothing of the old creation, the old kingdom or the old world can be transferred to the new. It is a question now of these two rival realms, and of which realm we belong to.

The apostle Paul, of course, leaves us in no doubt as to which of these two realms is now in fact ours. He tells us that God, in redemption, "delivered us out of the power of darkness, and translated us into the kingdom of the Son of his love" (Col. 1:12–13). our citizenship henceforth is *there*.

But in order to bring us into his new kingdom, God must do something new in us. He must make of us new creatures. Unless we are created anew we can never fit into the new realm. "That which is born of the flesh is flesh"; and, "flesh and blood cannot inherit the kingdom of God; neither doth corruption inherit incorruption" (John 3:16; 1 Cor. 15:50). However educated, however cultured, however improved it be, flesh is still flesh. Our fitness for the new kingdom is determined by the creation to which we belong. Do we belong to the old creation or the new? Are we born of the flesh or of the Spirit? Our ultimate suitability for the new realm hinges on the question of origin. The question is not "good or bad" but "flesh or Spirit"? "That which is born of the flesh *is* flesh," and it will never be anything else. That which is of the old creation can never pass over into the new.

Once we really understand what God is seeking, namely, something altogether new for himself, then we shall see clearly that we can never bring any contribution from the old realm into that new thing. God wanted to have us for himself, but he could not bring us as we were into that which he had purposed; so he first did away with us by the Cross of Christ, and then by resurrection provided a new life for us. "If any man is in Christ, he is a new creature (marginal reading: "there is a new creation"): the old things are passed away; behold, they are become new" (2 Cor. 5:17). Being now new creatures with a new nature and a new set of faculties, we can enter the new kingdom and the new world.

The Cross was the means God used to bring to an end "the old things" by setting aside altogether our "old man," and the resurrection was the means he employed to impart to us all that was necessary for our life in that new world.

> We were buried therefore with him through baptism into death: that like as Christ was raised from the dead through the glory of the Father, so we also might walk in newness of life (Rom. 6:4).

The greatest negative in the universe is the Cross, for with it God wiped out everything that was not of himself: the greatest positive in the universe is the resurrection, for through it God brought into being all he will have in the new sphere. So the resurrection stands at the threshold of the new creation. It is a blessed thing to see that the Cross ends all that belongs to the first regime, and that the resurrection introduces all that pertains to the second. Everything that had its beginning before resurrection must be wiped out. Resurrection is God's new starting-point.

We have now two worlds before us, the old and the new. In the old, Satan has absolute dominion. You may be a good man in the old creation, but as long as you belong to the old, you are under sentence of death, because nothing of the old can be carried over to the new. The Cross is God's declaration that all is of the old creation must die. Nothing of the first Adam can pass beyond the Cross; it all ends there. The sooner we see that, the better, for it is by the Cross that God has made a way of escape for us from that old creation. God gathered up in the person of his Son all that was of Adam and crucified him; so in him all that was of Adam was done away. Then God made, as it were, a proclamation throughout the universe saying:

> Through the Cross I have set aside all that is not of me; you who belong to the old creation are all included in that; you too have been crucified with Christ!

None of us can escape that verdict.

This brings us to the subject of baptism.

> Are ye ignorant that all we, who were baptized into Christ Jesus, were baptized into his death? We were buried therefore with him through baptism into death (Rom. 6:3–4).

We must now ask ourselves: "What is the significance of these words?"

Baptism in Scripture is associated with salvation. "He that believeth and is baptized shall be saved" (Mark 16:16). We cannot speak scripturally of "baptismal regeneration," but we may speak of "baptismal salvation." What is salvation? It relates not to our sins nor to the power of sin, but to the *cosmos* or world-system. We are involved in Satan's world-system. To be saved is to make our exit from his world-system into God's.

In the Cross of our Lord Jesus Christ, says Paul, "the world hath been crucified unto me, and I unto the world" (Gal. 6:14). This is the figure developed by Peter when he writes of the eight souls who were "saved through water" (1 Peter 3:20). Entering into the ark, Noah and those with him stepped by faith out of that old corrupt world into a new one. It was not so much that they were personally not drowned, but that they were *out* of that corrupt system. That is salvation.

Then Peter goes on: "Which also after a true likeness (marginal reading: 'in the antitype') doth now save you, even baptism" (verse 21). In other words, by that aspect of the Cross which is figured in baptism, you are delivered from this present evil world, and, by your baptism in water, you confirm this. It is baptism "into his death," ending one creation; but it is also baptism "into Christ Jesus," having in view a new one (Rom. 6:3). You go down into the water and your world, in figure, goes down with you. You come up in Christ, but your world is drowned.

"Believe on the Lord Jesus, and thou shalt be saved," said Paul at Philippi, and "spake the word of the Lord" to the jailer and his household. And he "was baptized, he and all his, immediately" (Acts 16:31–34). In doing so, he and those with him testified before God, his people and the spiritual powers that they were indeed saved from a world under judgment. As a result, we read, they rejoiced greatly, "having believed in God."

Thus it is clear that baptism is no mere question of a cup of water, nor even of a baptistry of water. It is something far greater, relating as it does both to the death and to the resurrection of our Lord; and having in view two worlds. Anyone who has seen men turn to Christ in a pagan country knows what tremendous issues are raised by baptism.

Burial Means an End

Peter goes on now to describe baptism in the passage just quoted as "the answer of a good conscience toward God" (1 Peter 3:21 AV). Now we cannot answer without being spoken to. If God had said nothing, we should have no need to answer. But he has spoken; he has spoken to us by the Cross. By it he has told of his judgment of us, of the world, of the old creation and of the old kingdom. The Cross is not only Christ's personally—an "individual" Cross. It is an all inclusive Cross, a "corporate" Cross, a Cross that includes you and me. God has put us all into his Son, and crucified us in him. In the last Adam he has wiped out all that was of the first Adam.

Now what is my answer to God's verdict on the old creation? I answer by asking for baptism. Why? In Romans 6:4, Paul explains that baptism means burial: "We were buried therefore with him through baptism." Baptism is of course connected with both death and resurrection, though in itself it is neither death nor resurrection: it is burial. But who qualifies for burial? Only the dead! So if I ask for baptism, I proclaim myself dead and fit only for the grave.

Alas, some have been taught to look on burial as a *means* to death; they try to die by getting themselves buried! Let me say emphatically that, unless our eyes have been opened by God to see that we have died in Christ and been buried with him, we have no right to be baptized. The reason we step down into the water is that we have recognized that in God's sight, we have *already* died. It is to that, that we testify. God's question is clear and simple. "Christ has died, and I have included you there. Now, what are you going to say to that?" What is my answer? "Lord, I believe you have done the crucifying. I say 'Yes' to the death and to the burial to which you have committed me." He has consigned me to death and the grave; by my request for baptism I give public assent to that fact.

In China a woman lost her husband, but, becoming deranged by her loss, she flatly refused to have him buried. Day after day for a fortnight he lay in the house. "No," she said, "he is not dead; I talk with him every night." She was unwilling to have him buried because, poor woman, she did not believe him to be dead. When are we willing to bury our dear ones? Only when we are absolutely sure that they have passed away. While there is the tiniest hope that they are alive we will never bury them. So when will I ask for baptism? When I see that God's way is perfect and that I deserved to die, and when I truly believe that God has already crucified me. Once I am fully persuaded that, before God, I am quite dead, then I apply for baptism. I say, "Praise God, I am dead! Lord, you have slain me; now get me buried!"

In China we have two emergency services, a "Red Cross" and a "Blue Cross." The first deals with those who are wounded in battle but are still alive, to bring them succor and healing; the second deals with those who are already dead in famine, flood, or war, to give them burial. God's dealings with us in the Cross of Christ are more drastic than those of the "Red Cross." He does not set out to patch up the old creation. By him even the still living are condemned to death and to burial, that they may be raised again to new life. God has done the work of crucifixion so that now we are counted among the dead; but we must accept this and submit to the work of the "Blue Cross," by sealing that death with "burial."

There is an old world and a new world, and between the two there is a tomb. God has already crucified me, but I must consent to be consigned to the tomb. My baptism confirms God's sentence, passed upon me in the Cross of his Son. It affirms that I am cut off from the old world and belong now to the new. So baptism is no small thing. It means for me a definite conscious break with the old way of life. This is the meaning of Romans 6:2: "We who died to sin, how shall we any longer live therein?" Paul asks, in effect, "If you would continue in the old world, why be baptized? You should never have been baptized if you meant to live on in the old realm." When once we see this, we are ready enough to clear the ground for the new creation by our assent to the burial of the old.

In Romans 6:5, still writing to those who "were baptized" (verse 3), Paul speaks of our being "united with Him by the likeness of his death." For by baptism we acknowledge in a figure that God has wrought an intimate union between ourselves and Christ in this matter of death and resurrection. One day I was seeking to emphasize to a Christian brother the intimacy of this union. We happened to be drinking tea together, so I took a lump of sugar and stirred it into my tea. A couple of minutes later I asked, "Can you tell me where the sugar is now, and where the tea?" "No," he said, "you have put them together and the one has become lost in the other; they cannot now be separated." It was a simple illustration, but it helped him to see the intimacy and the finality of our union with Christ in death. It is God that has put us there, and God's acts cannot be reversed.

What, in fact does this union imply? The real meaning behind baptism is that in the Cross we were "baptized" *into the historic death of Christ,* so that his death became ours. Our death and his became then so closely identified that it is impossible to divide between them. It is to this historic "baptism"—this God-wrought union with him—that we assent when we go down into the water. Our public testimony in baptism today is our admission that the death of Christ two thousand years ago was a mighty all-inclusive death, mighty enough and all-inclusive enough to carry away in it and bring to an end everything in us that is not of God.

Resurrection Unto Newness of Life

"If we have become united with him by the likeness of his death, we shall be also by the likeness of his resurrection" (Rom. 6:5).

Now with resurrection, the figure is different because something new is introduced. I am "baptized into his death," but I do not enter in quite the same way into his resurrection, for, praise the Lord! His resurrection enters into me, imparting to me a new life. In the death of the Lord, the emphasis is solely upon "I in Christ." With the resurrection, while the same thing is true, there is now a new emphasis upon "Christ in me." How is it possible for Christ to communicate His resurrection life to me? How do I receive this new life? Paul suggests, I think, a very good illustration with these very same words: "united with him." For the word "united" (AV "planted together") may carry in the Greek the sense of "grafted,"[1] and it gives us a very beautiful picture of the life of Christ which is imparted to us through resurrection.

In Fukien I once visited a man who owned an orchard of *long-ien*[2] trees. He had three or four acres of land and about three hundred fruit trees. I inquired if his trees had been grafted or if they were of the original native stock. "Do you think," he replied, "that I would waste my land growing ungrafted trees? What value could I ever expect from the old stock?

So I asked him to explain the process of grafting, which he gladly did. "When a tree has grown to a certain height," he said, "I lop off the top and

---

[1] Greek *sumphtuos* "planted or grown along with," "united with." The word is used in the sense of "grafted" in classical Greek. In the delightful illustration which follows, the analogy of grafting should perhaps not be pressed too closely, for it is not quite safe to imply, without some qualification, that Christ is grafted into the old stock. But what parable can adequately describe the miracle of the new creation?—*Angus Kinnear*

[2] *long-ien (Euphoria longana)* is a tree native to China. Its fruit resembles an apricot in size and has a round central stone, a dry, light brown, papery skin and a delicious white, grape-like pulp. It is eaten either fresh or dried, and is prized by the Chinese both for its flavour and for its food value.—*Angus Kinnear*

graft on to it." Pointing to a special tree he asked, "Do you see that tree? I call it the father tree, because all the grafts for the other trees are taken from that one. If the other trees were just left to follow the course of nature, their fruit would be only about the size of a raspberry, and would consist mainly of thick skin and seeds. This tree, from which the grafts for all the others are taken, bears a luscious fruit the size of a plum, with very thin skin and a tiny seed; and of course all the grafted trees bear fruit like it." "How does it happen?" I asked. "I simply take a little of the nature of the one tree and transfer it to the other," he explained. "I make a cleavage in the poor tree and insert a slip from the good one. Then I bind it up and leave it to grow." "But how can it grow?" I asked. "I don't know," he said, "but it does grow."

Then he showed me a tree bearing miserably poor fruit from the old stock below the graft, and rich juicy fruit from the new stock above the graft. "I have left the old shoots with their useless fruit on them to show the difference," he said. "From it you can understand the value of grafting. You can appreciate, can you not, why I grow only grafted trees?"

How can one tree bear the fruit of another? How can a poor tree bear good fruit? Only by grafting. Only by our implanting into it the life of a good tree. But if a man can graft a branch of one tree into another, cannot God take of the life of his Son and, so to speak, graft it into us?

A Chinese woman burned her arm badly and was taken to a hospital. In order to prevent serious contracture[3] due to scarring, it was found necessary to graft some new skin over the injured area, but the doctor attempted in vain to graft a piece of the woman's own skin onto the arm. Owing to her age and ill-nourishment, the skin graft was too poor and would not "take." Then a foreign nurse offered a piece of skin and the operation was carried out successfully. The new skin knit with the old, and the woman left the hospital with her arm perfectly healed; but there remained a patch of white foreign skin on her yellow arm to tell the tale of the past. You ask how the skin of another grew on that woman's arm? I do not know how it grew, but I know that it did grow.

---

[3] Contracture: an abnormal, often permanent shortening, as of muscle or scar tissue, that results in distortion or deformity, especially of a joint of the body. (*American Heritage Stedman's Medical Dictionary,* 2002, 2001, 1995.)

If an earthly surgeon can take a piece of skin from one human body and graft it on another,[4] cannot the Divine Surgeon implant the life of his Son into me? I do not know how it is done.

> The wind bloweth where it listeth, and thou hearest the voice thereof, but knowest not whence it cometh, and whither it goeth; so is every one that is born of the Spirit (John 3:8).

We cannot tell *how* God has done his work in us, but it is done. We can do nothing and need do nothing to bring it about, for by the resurrection God has already done it.

God has done everything. There is only one fruitful life in the world and that has been grafted into millions of other lives. We call this the "new birth." New birth is the reception of a life which I did not possess before. It is not that my natural life has been changed at all; it is that another life, a life altogether new, altogether divine, has become my life.

God has cut off the old creation by the Cross of his Son in order to bring in a new creation in Christ by resurrection. He has shut the door to that old kingdom of darkness and translated me into the kingdom of his dear Son. My glorying is in the fact that it has been done—that, through the Cross of our Lord Jesus Christ , that old world *has* " been crucified unto me, and I unto the world" (Galatians 6:14). My baptism is my public testimony to that fact. By it, as by my oral witness, my "confession is made unto salvation" (Romans 10:10).

---

[4] Whatever question medical men may raise as to the account of this unusual incident, the statement which follows is *not* open to challenge.—*Angus Kinnear*

CHAPTER 6

The Path of Progress: Presenting Ourselves to God

Our study has now brought us to the point where we are able to consider the true nature of consecration. We have before us the second half of Romans 6, from verse 12 to the end. In Romans 6:12–13 we read:

> Let not sin therefore reign in your mortal body, that ye should obey the lusts thereof: neither present your members unto sin as instruments of unrighteousness; but present yourselves unto God, as alive from the dead, and your members as instruments of righteousness unto God.

The operative word here is "present," and this occurs five times in the chapter, in verses 13, 16, and 19.[1]

Many have taken this word "present" to imply consecration, without looking carefully into its content. Of course that is what it does mean, but

---

[1] Note: Two Greek verbs, *paristano* and *paristemi*, are translated in these verses by "present" in the RV, where the AV has "yield." *Paristemi* occurs frequently with this meaning, e.g. in Rom. 12:1; 2 Cor. 11:2; Col. 1:22, 28, and in Luke 2:22 where it is used of the presenting of the infant Jesus to God in the Temple. Both words have an active sense, for which the RV translation "present" is greatly to be preferred. "Yield" contains a passive idea of "surrender" that has coloured much evangelical thought, but which is not in keeping with the context here in Romans.—*Angus Kinnear*

not in the sense in which we so often understand it. It is not the consecration of our "old man," with his instincts and resources—his natural wisdom, strength and other gifts—to the Lord for Him to use.

This will be at once clear from verse 13. Note there the clause, "as alive from the dead." Paul says: "Present yourselves unto God, as alive from the dead." This defines for us the point at which consecration begins. For what is here referred to is not the consecration of anything belonging to the old creation, but only of that which has passed through death to resurrection. The "presenting" spoken of is the outcome of my knowing my old man to be crucified. Knowing, reckoning, presenting to God: that is the divine order.

When I really know I am crucified with him, then spontaneously I reckon myself dead (verses 6 and 11); and when I know that I am raised with him from the dead, then likewise I reckon myself "alive unto God in Christ Jesus" (verses 9 and 11), for both the death and the resurrection side of the Cross are to be accepted by faith. When this point is reached, giving myself to him follows. In resurrection he is the source of my life—indeed he *is* my life; so I cannot but present everything to him, for all is his, not mine. But without passing through death, I have nothing to consecrate, nor is there anything God can accept, for he has condemned all that is of the old creation to the Cross. Death has cut off all that *cannot* be consecrated to him, and resurrection alone has made consecration possible. Presenting myself to God means that henceforth I consider my whole life as belonging to him.

The Third Step: "Present Yourselves . . . "

Let us observe that this "presenting" relates to the members of my body—that body which, as we saw earlier, is now unemployed in respect to sin. "Present yourselves . . . and your members," says Paul, and again: "Present your members" (Romans 6:13, 19). God requires of me that I now regard all my members, all my faculties, as belonging wholly to him.

It is a great thing when I discover I am no longer my own, but his. If the ten shillings in my pocket belong to me, then I have full authority over them. But if they belong to another who has committed them to me in trust, then I cannot buy what I please with them, and I dare not lose them.

Real Christian life begins with knowing this. How many of us know that, because Christ is risen, we are therefore alive "unto God" *and not unto ourselves?* How many of us dare not use our time or money or talents as we would, because we realize they are the Lord's, not ours? How many of us have such a strong sense that we belong to Another that we dare not squander a shilling of our money, or an hour of our time, or any of our mental or physical powers?

On one occasion a Chinese brother was traveling by train and found himself in a carriage together with three non-Christians who, in order to while away the time, wished to play cards. Lacking a fourth to complete the game, they invited this brother to join them. "I am sorry to disappoint you," he said, "but I cannot join your game, for I have not brought my hands with me." "Whatever do you mean?" they asked in blank astonishment. "This pair of hands does not belong to me," he said, and then there followed the explanation of the transfer of ownership that had taken place in his life. That brother regarded the members of his body as belonging entirely to the Lord. That is true holiness.

Paul says, "Present your members as servants to righteousness unto sanctification (AV 'holiness')" (Romans 6:19). Make it a definite act. "Present yourselves unto God."

Separated Unto the Lord

What is holiness? Many people think we become holy by the eradication of something evil within. No, we become holy by being separated unto God. In Old Testament times, it was when a man was chosen by God to be altogether His, that he was publicly anointed with oil and was then said to be "sanctified." Thereafter he was regarded as *set apart* to God. In the same manner even animals or material things—a lamb, or the gold of the temple—could be sanctified, not by the eradication of anything evil in them, but by being thus reserved exclusively to the Lord. "Holiness" in the Hebrew sense meant something thus set apart, and all true holiness is holiness "to the Lord" (Exodus 28:36). I give myself over wholly to Christ: that is holiness.

Presenting myself to God implies a recognition that I am altogether his. This giving of myself is a definite thing, just as definite as reckoning.

There must be a day in my life when I pass out of my own hands into his, and from that day forward I belong to him and no longer to myself. That does not mean that I consecrate myself to be a preacher or a missionary. Alas, many people are missionaries not because they have truly consecrated themselves to God, but because, in the sense of which we are speaking, they have *not* consecrated themselves to him. They have "consecrated" (as they would put it) something altogether different, namely, their own uncrucified natural faculties to the doing of his work; but that is not true consecration. Then to what are we to be consecrated? Not to Christian work, but *to the will of God to be and do whatever he requires.*

David had many mighty men. Some were generals and others were gatekeepers, according as the king assigned them their task. We must be willing to be either generals or gatekeepers, allotted to our parts just as God wills and not as we choose. If you are a Christian, then God has marked out a pathway for you—a "course" as Paul calls it in 2 Timothy 4:7. Not only Paul's path but the path of every Christian has been clearly marked out by God, and it is of supreme importance that each one should know and walk in the God-appointed course. "Lord, I give myself to thee with this desire alone, to know and walk in the path thou hast ordained." That is true giving. If at the close of a life we can say with Paul: "I have finished my course," then we are blessed indeed. There is nothing more tragic than to come to the end of life and know we have been on the wrong course. We have only one life to live down here, and we are free to do as we please with it, but if we seek our own pleasure, our life will never glorify God. A devoted Christian once said in my hearing, "I want nothing for myself; I want everything for God." Do you want anything apart from God, or does all your desire center in his will? Can you truly say that the will of God is "good and acceptable and perfect" *to you?* (Romans 12:2)

For it is our wills that are in question here. That strong self-assertive will of mine must go to the Cross, and I must give myself over wholly to the Lord. We cannot expect a tailor to make us a coat if we do not give him any cloth, nor a builder to build us a house if we let him have no building material; and in just the same way we cannot expect the Lord to live out his life in us, if we do not give him our lives in which to live. Without reservations, without controversy, we must give ourselves to him to do as he pleases with us. "Present yourselves unto God" (Romans 6:13).

Servant or Slave?

If we give ourselves unreservedly to God, many adjustments may have to be made: in family, or business, or church relationships, or in the matter of our personal views. God will not let anything of ourselves remain. His finger will touch, point by point, everything that is not of him, and he will say: "This must go." Are you willing? It is foolish to resist God, and always wise to submit to him. We admit that many of us still have controversies with the Lord. He wants something, while we want something else. Many things we dare not look into, dare not pray about, dare not even think about, lest we lose our peace. We can evade the issue in that way, but to do so will bring us out of the will of God. It is always an easy matter to get out of his will, but it is a blessed thing just to hand ourselves over to him and let him have his way with us.

How good it is to have the consciousness that we belong to the Lord and are not our own! There is nothing more precious in the world. It is that which brings the awareness of his continual presence, and the reason is obvious. I must first have the sense of God's possession of me, before I can have the sense of his presence with me. When once his ownership is established, then I dare do nothing in my own interests, for I am his exclusive property. "Know ye not, that to whom ye present yourselves as servants unto obedience, his servants ye are whom ye obey?" (Romans 6:16) The word here rendered "servant" really signifies a bondservant, a slave. This word is used several times in the second half of Romans 6. What is the difference between a servant and a slave? A servant may serve another, but the ownership does not pass to that other. If he likes his master, he can serve him, but if he does not like him, he can give in his notice and seek another master. Not so is it with the slave. He is not only the servant of another but he is the possession of another. How did I become the slave of the Lord? On his part he bought me, and on my part I presented myself to him. By right of redemption I am God's property, but if I would be his slave I must willingly give myself to him, for he will never compel me to do so.

The trouble with many Christians today is that they have an insufficient idea of what God is asking of them. How glibly they say: "Lord, I am willing for anything." Do you know that God is asking of you your very life? There are cherished ideals, strong wills, precious relationships, much-loved work, that will have to go; so do not give yourself to God unless you mean it. God will take you seriously, even if you did not mean it seriously.

When the Galilian boy brought his bread to the Lord, what did the Lord do with it? He broke it. God will always break what is offered to him. He breaks what he takes, but after breaking it he blesses and uses it to meet the needs of others. After you give yourself to the Lord, he begins to break what was offered to him. Everything seems to go wrong, and you protest and find fault with the ways of God. But to stay there is to be no more than just a broken vessel—no good for the world because you have gone too far for the world to use you, and no good for God either because you have not gone far enough for him to use you. You are out of gear with the world, and you have a controversy with God. This is the tragedy of many a Christian.

My giving of myself to the Lord must be an initial fundamental act. Then day by day I must go on giving to him, not finding fault with his use of me, but accepting with praise even what the flesh finds hard. That way lies true enrichment.

I am the Lord's and now no longer reckon myself to be my own, but acknowledge in everything his ownership and authority. That is the attitude God delights in, and to maintain it is true consecration. I do not consecrate myself to be a missionary or a preacher; I consecrate myself to God to do his will where I am, be it in school, office, or kitchen, wherever he may, in his wisdom, send me. Whatever he ordains for me is sure to be the very best, for nothing but good can come to those who are wholly his.

May we always be possessed by the consciousness that we are not our own.

CHAPTER 7

The Eternal Purpose

We have spoken of the need of revelation, of faith and of consecration, if we are to live the normal Christian life. But unless we see the end God has in view, we shall never clearly understand why these steps are necessary to lead us to that end. So before we consider further the question of inward experience, let us first look at the great divine goal before us.

What is God's purpose in creation and what is his purpose in redemption? It may be summed up in two phrases, one from each of our two sections of Romans. It is: "The glory of God," (Romans 3:23) and "The glory of the children of God" (Romans 8:21).

In Romans 3:23 we read: "All have sinned, and fall short of the glory of God." God's purpose for man was glory, but sin thwarted that purpose by causing man to miss God's glory. When we think of sin, we instinctively think of the judgment it brings; we invariably associate it with condemnation and hell. Man's thought is always of the punishment that will come to him if he sins, but God's thought is always of the glory man will miss if he sins. The result of sin is that we forfeit God's glory: the result of redemption is that we are qualified again for glory. God's purpose in redemption is glory, glory, glory.

Firstborn Among Many Brethren

This consideration takes us forward into Romans chapter 8, where the topic is developed in verses 16 to 18 and again in verses 29 and 30. Paul says:

> We are children of God: and if children, then heirs; heirs of God, and joint-heirs with Christ; if so be that we suffer with him, that we may be also glorified with him. For I reckon that the sufferings of this present time are not worthy to be compared with the glory which shall be revealed to usward. (Romans 8:16–18)

and again:

> Whom he foreknew, he also foreordained to be conformed to the image of his Son, that he might be the firstborn among many brethren: and whom he foreordained, them he also called: and whom he called, them he also justified: and whom he justified, them he also glorified. (Romans 8:29–30)

What was God's objective? It was that his Son Jesus Christ might be the firstborn among many brethren, all of whom should be conformed to his image. How did God realize that objective? "Whom he justified, them he also glorified." Thus, God's purpose in creation and redemption was to make Christ the firstborn Son among many glorified sons. That may perhaps at first convey very little to many of us, but let us look into it more carefully.

In John 1:14 we are told that the Lord Jesus was God's only begotten Son: "the Word became flesh, and dwelt among us (and we beheld his glory, glory as of the only begotten from the Father)." That he was God's only begotten Son signifies that God had no other but this one. He was with the Father from all eternity. But, we are told, God was not satisfied that Christ should remain the only begotten Son; he wanted also to make him his first begotten. How could an only begotten Son become a first begotten? The answer is simple: by the Father having more children. If you have but one son then he is the only begotten, but if thereafter you have other children, then the only begotten becomes the first begotten.

The divine purpose in creation and redemption was that God should have many children. He wanted *us*, and could not be satisfied without us.

Some time ago I called to see Mr. George Cutting[1], the writer of the well-known tract *Safety, Certainty, and Enjoyment.* When I was ushered into the presence of this old saint of ninety-three years, he took my hand in his and in a quiet, deliberate way he said: "Brother, do you know, I cannot do without him? And do you know, he cannot do without me?" Though I was with him for over an hour, his great age and physical frailty made any sustained conversation impossible. But what remains in my memory of that interview was his frequent repetition of these two questions: "Brother, do you know, I cannot do without him? And do you know, he *cannot do without me?"*

In reading the story of the prodigal son, most people are impressed with all the troubles the prodigal meets; they are occupied in thinking what a bad time he is having. But that is not the point of the parable. "My son . . . was lost, and is found"—there is the heart of the story. It is not a question of what the son suffers, but of what the Father loses. *He* is the sufferer; *he* is the loser. A sheep is lost: whose is the loss? The shepherd's. A coin is lost: whose is the loss? The woman's. A son is lost: whose is the loss? The Father's. That is the lesson of Luke chapter 15.

The Lord Jesus was the only begotten Son, and as the only begotten, he had no brothers. But the Father sent the Son in order that the only begotten might also be the first begotten, and the beloved Son have many brethren. There you have the whole story of the Incarnation and the Cross; and there you have at the last the purpose of God fulfilled in his "bringing many sons unto glory" (Heb. 2:10).

In Romans 8:29 we read of "many brethren"; in Hebrews 10, of "many sons." From the point of view of the Lord Jesus, they are "brethren"; from the point of view of God the Father, they are "sons." Both words in this context convey the idea of maturity. God is seeking full-grown sons; but he does not stop even there. For he does not want his sons to live in a barn or a garage or a field; he wants them in his home; he wants them to share his glory. That is the explanation of Romans 8:30: "Whom he justified, them he also glorified." Sonship—the full expression of his Son—is God's goal in the many sons. How could he bring that about? By justifying them and then by glorifying them. In

---

[1] George Cutting (1834-1934) wrote a great deal on the Christian life. His works include at least 35 other booklets, among them *Light For Anxious Souls, Are You a Member? And of What?,* and *The Old Nature and New Birth, or: The New Convert and His Difficulties.*

his dealings with them, God will never stop short of that goal. He set himself to have sons, and to have those sons, mature and responsible, with him in glory. He made provision for the whole of Heaven to be peopled with glorified sons. That was his purpose in the redemption of mankind.

The Grain of Wheat

But how could God's only begotten Son become his first begotten? The method is explained in John 12:24: "Verily, verily, I say unto you, 'Except a grain of wheat fall into the earth and die, it abideth by itself alone; but if it die, it beareth much fruit.'"

Who was that grain? It was the Lord Jesus. In the whole universe God put his one grain of wheat into the ground and it died, and in resurrection the only begotten grain became the first begotten grain, and from the one grain there have sprung many grains.[2]

In respect of his divinity, the Lord Jesus remains uniquely "the only begotten Son of God." Yet there is a sense in which, from the resurrection onward through all eternity, he is also the first begotten, and his life from that time is found in many brethren. For we who are born of the Spirit are made thereby "partakers of the divine nature" (2 Peter 1:4), though not, mark you, as of ourselves, but only, as we shall see in a moment, in dependence upon God and by virtue of our being "in Christ." We have, "received the spirit of adoption, whereby we cry, 'Abba, Father.' The Spirit himself beareth witness with our spirit, that we are children of God" (Rom. 8:15, 16).

It was by way of the Incarnation and the Cross that the Lord Jesus made this possible. Therein was the Father-heart of God satisfied, for in the Son's obedience unto death, the Father has secured his many sons.

The first and the twentieth chapters of John are in this respect most precious. In the beginning of his Gospel John tells us that Jesus was "the only begotten from the Father." At the end of his Gospel he tells us how, after the He had died and risen again, he said to Mary Magdalene, "Go unto my brethren, and say to them, 'I ascend unto my Father and your Father, and my God and your God'" (John 20:17).

---

[2] In an earlier edition of *The Normal Christian Life*, this sentance read, perhaps more clearly: "In the whole universe God had only one 'grain of wheat'; he had no second grain. God put his one grain of wheat into the ground and it died, and in resurrection the only begotten grain became the first begotten grain, and from the one grain there have sprung many grains."

Hitherto in this Gospel the Lord had spoken often of "the Father" or of "my Father." Now, in resurrection, he adds, ". . . and your Father." It is the eldest Son, the first begotten, speaking. By his death and resurrection many brethren have been brought into God's family, and so, in the same verse, he uses this very name for them, calling them, "my brethren." By doing this, He affirms that "He is not ashamed to call them brethren" (Heb. 2:11).

The Choice that Confronted Adam

God planted a great number of trees in the garden of Eden, but "in the midst of the garden"—that is, in a place of special prominence—he planted two trees: the tree of life and the tree of the knowledge of good and evil. Adam was created innocent; he had no knowledge of good and evil. Think of a grown man, say thirty years old, who has no sense of right or wrong, no power to differentiate between the two! Would you not say such a man was undeveloped? Well, that is exactly what Adam was. And God brings him into the garden and says to him, in effect,

> Now the garden is full of trees, full of fruits, and of the fruit of every tree you may eat freely. But in the very midst of the garden is one tree called "the tree of the knowledge of good and evil"; you must not eat of that, for in the day that you do so you will surely *die*. But remember, the name of the other tree close by is *Life*.

What, then, is the meaning of these two trees? Adam was, so to speak, created morally neutral—neither sinful nor holy, but innocent—and God put those two trees there so that he might exercise free choice. He could choose the tree of life, or he could choose the tree of the knowledge of good and evil.

Now the knowledge of good and evil, though forbidden to Adam, is not wrong in itself. Without it, however, Adam is in a sense limited, in that he cannot decide *for himself* on moral issues. Judgment of right and wrong resides not in him but in God, and Adam's only course when faced with any question is to refer it to Jehovah God. Thus you have a life in the garden which is totally dependent on God. These two trees, then, typify two deep principles; they represent two planes of life, the divine and the human. The "tree of life" is God himself, for God is life. He is the highest form of life, and he is also the source and goal of life. And the fruit: what is that? It is our Lord Jesus Christ. You cannot eat the tree, but you can eat the fruit. No one is able to receive God as God, but we can receive the Lord Jesus. The fruit is the edible part, the receivable part of the tree. So—may I say it reverently?—the Lord Jesus is really God in a receivable form. God in Christ, we can receive.

If Adam should take of the tree of life, he would partake of the life of God. Thus he would become a "son" of God, in the sense of having in him a life that derived from God. There you would have God's life in union with man: a race of men having the life of God in them and *living in constant dependence upon God for that life*. But if instead, Adam should turn the other way and take the fruit of the tree of the knowledge of good and evil, then he would develop his own manhood along natural lines apart from God. As a self-sufficient being, he would have the power in himself to form independent judgment, *but he would have no life from God.*

So this was the alternative that lay before him. Choosing the way of the Spirit, the way of obedience, he could become a "son" of God, living in dependence upon God for his life; or, taking the natural course, he could put the finishing touch to himself, as it were, by becoming a self-dependent being, judging and acting apart from God. The history of humanity is the outcome of the choice he made.

Adam's Choice the Reason for the Cross

Adam chose the tree of the knowledge of good and evil, and thereby took up independent ground. In doing so he became (as men are now in their own eyes) a "fully developed" man. He could command a knowledge; he could decide for himself; he could go on or stop. From then on he was "wise" (Genesis 3:6). But the consequence for him was death rather than life, because the choice he had made involved complicity with Satan and brought him therefore under the judgment of God. That is why access to the tree of life had thereafter to be forbidden to him.

Two planes of life had been set before Adam: that of divine life in dependence upon God, and that of human life with its "independent" resources. Adam's choice of the latter was sin, because thereby he allied himself with Satan to thwart the eternal purpose of God. He did so by choosing to develop his manhood—to become perhaps a very fine man, even by his standards a "perfect" man—apart from God. But the end was death, because he had not in him the divine life necessary to realize God's purpose in his being, but had chosen to become instead an "independent" agent of the Enemy. Thus in Adam we all become sinners, equally dominated by Satan, equally subject to the law of sin and death, and equally deserving of the wrath of God.

From this we see the divine reason for the death and resurrection of the Lord Jesus. We see too the divine reason for true consecration—for reckoning ourselves to be dead unto sin but alive unto God in Christ Jesus, and for presenting ourselves unto him as alive from the dead. We must all go to the Cross, because *what is in us by nature is a self-life,* subject to the law of sin. Adam chose a self-life rather than a divine life; so God had to gather up all that was in Adam and do away with it. Our "old man" has been crucified. God has put us all in Christ and crucified him as the last Adam, and thus all that is of Adam has passed away.

Then Christ arose in new form; with a body still, but "in the Spirit," no longer "in the flesh." "The last Adam became a life-giving spirit" (1 Cor. 15:45). The Lord Jesus now has a resurrected body, a spiritual body, a glorious body, and since he is no longer in the flesh, he can now be received by all. "He that eateth me, he also shall live because of me," said Jesus (John 6:57). The Jews revolted at the thought of eating his flesh and drinking his blood, but of course they could not receive him then because he was still literally in the flesh. Now that he is in the Spirit, every one of us can receive him, and it is by partaking of his resurrection life that we are constituted children of God. "As many as received him, to them gave he the right to become children of God . . . which were born . . . of God." (John 1:12–13).

God is not out to reform our life. It is not his aim to bring that life to a certain stage of refinement, for it is on a totally wrong plane. On that plane he cannot now bring man to glory. He must have a *new* man; one born anew, born of God. Regeneration and justification go together.

He That Hath the Son Hath the Life

There are various planes of life. Human life lies between the life of the lower animals and the life of God. We cannot bridge the gulf that divides us from the plan above or the plan below, and the distance that separates us from the life of God is vastly greater than that which separates us from the life of the lower animals.

One day in China I called on a Christian leader who was sick in bed, and whom, for the sake of this story, I shall call "Mr. Wong" (though that was not his real name). He was a very learned man, a Doctor of Philosophy, and one esteemed throughout the whole of China for his high moral principles, and he had long been engaged in Christian work. But he did not believe in the need for regeneration; he only proclaimed a social gospel of love and good works.

When I called on Mr. Wong, his pet dog was by his bedside, and after speaking with him of the things of God and of the nature of his work in us, I pointed to the dog and inquired his name. He told me he was called Fido. "Is Fido his Christian name or his surname?" I asked (using the common Chinese terms for "personal name" and "family name"). "Oh, that is just his name," he said. "Do you mean that is just his Christian name? Can I call him Fido Wong?" I continued. "Certainly not!" came the emphatic reply. "But he lives in your family," I protested, "Why don't you call him Fido Wong?" Then, indicating his two daughters, I asked "Are your daughters not called Miss Wong?" "Yes!" "Well then, why cannot I call your dog Master Wong?" The Doctor laughed, and I went on:

> Do you see what I am getting at? Your daughters were born into your family and they bear your name because you have communicated your life to them. Your dog may be an intelligent dog, a well-behaved dog, and altogether a most remarkable dog; but the question is not, "Is he a good or a bad dog?" It is merely, "Is he a dog?" He does not need to be bad to be disqualified from being a member of your family; he only needs to be a dog. The same principle applies to you in your relationship to God. The question is not whether you are a bad man or a good man, more or less, but simply, "Are you a man?" If your life is on a lower plane than that of God's life, then you cannot belong to the divine family. Throughout your life your aim in preaching has been to turn bad men into good men; but men *as such*, whether good or bad, can have no vital relationship with God. Our only hope as men is to receive the Son of God, and when we do so, his life in us will constitute us sons of God.

The Doctor saw the truth, and that day he became a member of God's family by receiving the Son of God into his heart.

What we today possess in Christ is more than Adam lost. Adam was only a developed *man*. He remained on that plane, and never possessed the life of God. But when we receive the Son of God, not only do we receive the forgiveness of sins; we receive also the divine life which was represented in the garden by the tree of life. By the new birth we possess what Adam missed, for we receive a life he never had.

They Are All of One

God wants sons who shall be joint-heirs with Christ in glory. That is his goal; but how can he bring that about? Turn now to Hebrews 2:10–11:

> It became him, for whom are all things, and through whom are all things, in bringing many sons unto glory, to make the author of their salvation perfect through sufferings. For both he that sanctifieth and they that are sanctified are all of one: for which cause he is not ashamed to call them brethren.

There are two parties mentioned here, namely, "many sons" and "the author of their salvation," or, in different terms, "he that sanctifieth" and "they that are sanctified." But these two parties are said to be "all of one." The Lord Jesus as Man derived his life from God, and (in another sense, but just as truly) we derive our new life from God. He was "begotten . . . of the Holy Ghost" (Matthew 1:20, marg.), and we were "born of . . . . the spirit," "born . . . of God" (John 3:5; 1:13). So, God says, we are all of One. "Of" in the Greek means "out of." The first begotten Son and the many sons are all (though in different senses) "out of" the one Source of life. Do you realize that we have the same life today that God has? The life which he possesses in Heaven is the life which he has imparted to us here on the earth. That is the precious "gift of God" (Rom. 6:23). It is for this reason that we can live a life of holiness, for it is not our own life that has been changed, but the life of God that has been imparted to us.

Do you notice that, in this consideration of the eternal purpose, the whole question of sin ultimately goes out? It no longer has a place. Sin came in with Adam, and even when it has been dealt with, as it has to be, we are only brought back to the point where Adam was. But in relating us again to the divine purpose—in, as it were, restoring to us access to the tree of life—redemption has given us far more than Adam ever had. It has made us partakers of the very life of God himself.

CHAPTER 8

The Holy Spirit

We have spoken of the eternal purpose of God as the motive and explanation of all his dealings with us. Now, before we return to our study of the phases of Christian experience as set forth in Romans, we must digress yet again in order to consider something which lies at the heart of all our experience as the vitalizing power of effective life and service. I refer to the personal presence and ministry of the Holy Spirit of God.

And here, too, let us take as our starting-point two verses from Romans, one from each of our sections.

> The love of God hath been shed abroad in our hearts through the Holy Ghost which was given unto us (Romans 5:5).

And—

> If any man hath not the Spirit of Christ, he is none of His (Romans 8:9).

God does not give his gifts at random, nor dispense them in an arbitrary fashion. They are given freely to all, but they are given on a definite basis. God has truly "blessed us with every spiritual blessing in the heavenly places

79

in Christ" (Ephesians 1:3), but if those blessings which are ours in Christ are to become ours in experience, we must know on what grounds we can appropriate them.

In considering the gift of the Holy Spirit, it is helpful to think of this in two aspects: as the Spirit outpoured, and the Spirit indwelling—and our purpose now is to understand on what basis this twofold gift of the Holy Spirit becomes ours. I have no doubt that we are right in distinguishing thus between the outward and the inward manifestations of his working, and that as we go on we shall find the distinction helpful. Moreover, when we compare them, we cannot but come to the conclusion that the inward activity of the Holy Spirit is the more precious. But to say this, is not for one moment to imply that his outward activity is not also precious, for God only gives good gifts to his children.

Unfortunately we are apt to esteem our privileges lightly because of their sheer abundance. The Old Testament saints, who were not as favored as we are, could appreciate more readily than we do the preciousness of this gift of the outpoured Spirit. In their day it was a gift given only to a few—chiefly to priests, judges, kings and prophets—whereas now it is the portion of every child of God. Think! We who are mere nonentities can have the same Spirit resting upon us as rested upon Moses the friend of God, upon David the beloved king, and upon Elijah the mighty prophet. By receiving the gift of the outpoured Holy Spirit, we join the ranks of God's chosen servants of the Old Testament dispensation. Once we see the value of this gift of God, and realize too our deep need of it, we shall immediately ask, "How can I receive the Holy Spirit in this way to equip me with spiritual gifts and to empower me for God's service?" Upon what basis has the Spirit been given to His children?

The Spirit Outpoured

Let us turn first to Acts chapter 2, verses 32 to 36, and consider this passage briefly:

[32]This Jesus did God raise up, whereof we all are witnesses. [33]Being therefore by the right hand of God exalted, and having received of the Father the promise of the Holy Ghost, he hath poured forth this, which ye see and hear. [34]For David ascended not into the heavens: but he saith him-

self, The Lord said unto my Lord, sit thou on my right hand, [35]Till I make thine enemies the footstool of thy feet. [36]Let all the house of Israel therefore know assuredly, that God hath made him both Lord and Christ, this Jesus whom ye crucified.

We will set aside, for the moment, verses 34 and 35 and consider verses 33 and 36 together. The former are a quotation from the 110th Psalm and are really a parenthesis, so we shall get the force of Peter's argument better if we ignore them for the time being. In verse 33 Peter states that the Lord Jesus was exalted "at the right hand of God" (marg.). What was the result? He "received of the Father the promise of the Holy Ghost." And what followed? The miracle of Pentecost! The result of his exaltation was—"this, which ye see and hear."

Upon what basis, then, was the Spirit first given to the Lord Jesus to be poured out upon his people? It was upon the fact of his exaltation to Heaven. This passage makes it quite clear that the Holy Spirit was poured out because Jesus was exalted. The outpouring of the Spirit has no relation to your merits or mine, but only to the merits of the Lord Jesus. The question of what *we* are does not come into consideration at all here, but only what *he* is. He is glorified; therefore the Spirit is poured out.

Because the Lord Jesus died on the Cross, I have received forgiveness of sins; because the Lord Jesus rose from the dead, I have received new life; because the Lord Jesus has been exalted to the right hand of the Father, I have received the outpoured Spirit. All is because of him; nothing is because of me. Remission of sins is not based on human merit, but on the Lord's crucifixion; regeneration is not based on human merit, but on the Lord's resurrection; and the enduement with the Holy Spirit is not based on human merit, but on the Lord's exaltation. The Holy Spirit has not been poured out on you or me to prove how great we are, but to prove the greatness of the Son of God.

Now look at verse 36. There is a word here which demands our careful attention: the word "therefore." How is this word generally used? Not to introduce a statement, but to follow a statement that has already been made. Its use always implies that something has been mentioned before. Now what has preceded this particular "therefore"? With what is it connected? It cannot reasonably be connected with either verse 34 or verse

35, but it quite obviously relates back to verse 33. Peter has just referred to the outpouring of the Spirit upon the disciples "which ye see and hear," and he says: "Let all the house of Israel *therefore* know assuredly, that God hath made him both Lord and Christ, this Jesus whom ye crucified." Peter says, in effect, to his audience:

> This outpouring of the Spirit, which you have witnessed with your own eyes and ears, proves that Jesus of Nazareth whom ye crucified is now both Lord and Christ.

The Holy Spirit was poured out on earth to prove what had taken place in Heaven—the exaltation of Jesus of Nazareth to the right hand of God. The purpose of Pentecost is to prove the Lordship of Jesus Christ.

There was a young man named Joseph, who was dearly loved of his father. One day news reached the father of the death of his son, and for years Jacob lamented Joseph's loss. But Joseph was not in the grave; he was in a place of glory and power. After Jacob had been mourning the death of his son for years, it was suddenly reported to him that Joseph was alive and in a high position in Egypt. At first Jacob could not take it in. It was too good to be true. But ultimately he was persuaded that the story of Joseph's exaltation was really a fact. How did he come to believe in it? He went out, and saw the chariots that Joseph had sent from Egypt.

What do the chariots represent? They surely typify here the Holy Spirit, sent both to be the evidence that God's Son is in glory and to convey us there. How do we know that Jesus of Nazareth, who was crucified by wicked men nearly two thousand years ago, did not just die a martyr's death but is at the Father's right hand in glory? How can we know for a surety that he is Lord of lords and King of kings? We can know it beyond dispute because he has poured out his Spirit upon us. Hallelujah! Jesus *is* Lord! Jesus *is* Christ! Jesus of Nazareth *is* both Lord and Christ!

If the gift of the Spirit depends thus upon the exaltation of the Lord Jesus alone, is it possible then that *He* has been glorified and *you* have not received the Spirit? On what basis did you receive forgiveness of sins? Was it because you prayed so earnestly, or because you read your Bible from cover to cover, or because of your regular attendance at church? Was it because of your merits at all? No! A thousand times, no! On what grounds then were your sins forgiven? "Apart from shedding of blood there is no remission" (Hebrews 9:22). The sole grounds for forgiveness is the shedding of blood; and since the precious Blood has been shed, your sins have been forgiven.

Now the principle on which we receive the enduement of the Holy Spirit is the very same as that on which we receive forgiveness of sins. The Lord has been crucified, therefore our sins have been forgiven; the Lord has been glorified, therefore the Spirit has been poured out upon us. Is it possible that the Son of God shed his Blood and that your sins, dear child of God, have not been forgiven? Never! Then is it possible that the Son of God has been glorified and you have not received the Spirit? Never!

Some of you may say:

> I agree with all this, but I have no experience of it. Am I to sit down smugly and say I have everything, when I know perfectly well I have nothing?

No, we must never rest content with objective facts alone. We need subjective experience also; but that experience will only come as we rest upon divine facts. God's facts are the basis of our experience.

Let us go back again to the question of justification. How were you justified? Not by doing anything at all, but by accepting the fact that the Lord had done everything. Enduement with the Holy Spirit becomes yours in exactly the same way, not by your doing anything yourself, but by your putting your faith in what the Lord has already done.

If we lack the experience, we must ask God only for a revelation of the eternal fact of the baptism of the Holy Spirit as the gift of the exalted Lord to his Church. Once we see that, effort will cease, and prayer will give place to praise. It was a revelation of what the Lord had done for the world that brought to an end our efforts to secure forgiveness of sins, and it is a revelation of what the Lord has done for his Church that will bring to an end our efforts to secure the baptism of the Holy Spirit. We work because we have not seen the work of Christ. But when once we have seen that, faith will spring up in our hearts, and as we believe, experience will follow.

Some time ago a young man, who had only been a Christian for five weeks and who had formerly been violently opposed to the gospel, attended a series of meetings which I was addressing in Shanghai. At the close of one in which I was speaking along the above lines, he went home and began to pray earnestly,

> Lord, I do want the power of the Holy Spirit. Seeing thou hast now been glorified, wilt thou not now pour out thy Spirit upon me?

Then he corrected himself: "Oh no, Lord, that's all wrong!" and began to pray again:

> Lord Jesus, we are in a life-partnership, thou and I, and the Father has promised us two things—glory for thee, and the Spirit for me. Thou, Lord, hast received the glory; therefore it is unthinkable that I have not received the Spirit. Lord, I praise thee! Thou hast already received the glory, and I have already received the Spirit.

From that day the power of the Spirit was consciously upon him.

Faith Is Again the Key

As for forgiveness, so equally with the coming upon us of the Holy Spirit, the whole question is one of faith. As soon as we see the Lord Jesus on the Cross, we know our sins are forgiven; and as soon as we see the Lord Jesus on the Throne, we know the Holy Spirit has been poured out upon us. The basis upon which we receive the enduement of the Holy Spirit is not our praying and fasting and waiting, but the exaltation of Christ. Those who emphasize tarrying and hold "tarrying meetings" only mislead us, for the gift is not for the "favored few", but for all, because it is not given on the grounds of what we are at all, but of what Christ is. The Spirit has been poured out to prove His goodness and greatness, not ours. Christ has been crucified, therefore we have been forgiven: Christ has been glorified, therefore we have been endued with power from on high. It is all because of him.

Suppose an unbeliever expresses the desire to be saved, and you explain to him the way of salvation and pray with him. Suppose then he prays after this fashion: "Lord Jesus, I believe thou hast died for me, and that thou canst blot out all my sins. I truly believe thou wilt forgive me." Have you any confidence that that man is saved? When will you rest assured that he has really been born again? Not when he prays: "Lord, I believe thou *wilt* forgive my sins," but when he says: "Lord, I praise thee that Thou *hast* forgiven my sins. Thou *hast* died for me; therefore my sins *are* blotted out." You believe a person is saved when his prayer yields to praise, and from asking the Lord to forgive him, [instead] he turns to praising Him that He has *already* done so because the Blood of the Lamb has *already* been shed.

In the same way, you can pray and wait for years and never experience the Spirit's power; but when you cease to plead with the Lord to pour out his Spirit upon you, and when instead you trustfully praise him that the Spirit *has been* poured out because the Lord Jesus *has been* glorified, you will find that your problem is solved. Praise God! No single child of his needs agonize, nor even wait, for the Spirit to be given. Jesus is not *going to be made* Lord; he *is* Lord. Therefore I am not *going to receive* the Spirit; I *have received* the Spirit. It is all a question of the faith which comes by revelation. When our eyes are opened to see that the Spirit has already been poured out, because Jesus has already been glorified, then prayer turns to praise in our hearts.

All spiritual blessings come to us on a definite basis. God's gifts are freely given, but there are conditions to be fulfilled on our part before their reception is possible. There is a passage in God's Word which states the conditions of receiving the outpoured Spirit:

> Repent ye, and be baptized every one of you in the name of Jesus Christ unto the remission of your sins; and ye shall receive the gift of the Holy Ghost. For to you is the promise, and to your children, and to all that are afar off, even as many as the Lord our God shall call unto him (Acts 2:38–39).

Four things are mentioned here: Repentance, Baptism, Forgiveness, and the Holy Spirit. The first two are conditions, the second two are gifts. What are the conditions to be fulfilled if we are to have forgiveness of sins? According to this scripture, they are two: repentance and baptism.

The first condition is repentance, which means a change of mind. Formerly I thought sin a pleasant thing, but now I have changed my mind about it; formerly I thought the world an attractive place, but now I know better; formerly I regarded it a miserable business to be a Christian, but now I think differently. Once I thought certain things delightful, now I think them vile; once I thought other things utterly worthless, now I think them most precious. That is a change of mind, and that is repentance. No life can be truly changed apart from such a change of mind.

The second condition is baptism. Baptism is an outward expression of an inward faith. When in my heart I truly believe that I have died with Christ, have been buried and have risen with him, then I ask for baptism. I thereby declare publicly what I believe privately. Baptism is faith in action.

Here then are two divinely appointed conditions of forgiveness—repentance, and faith publicly expressed. Have you repented? Have you testified publicly to your union with your Lord? Then have you received remission of sins and the gift of the Holy Ghost? You say you have only received the first gift, not the second. But, my friend, God offered you two things if you fulfilled two conditions! Why have you only taken one? What are you doing about the second?

Suppose I went into a book-shop, selected a two-volume book, priced at ten shillings, and, having put down a ten-shilling note, walked out of the shop, carelessly leaving one volume on the counter. When I reached home and discovered the oversight, what do you think I should do? I should go straight back to the shop to get the forgotten book, but I should not dream of paying anything for it. I should simply remind the shopkeeper that both volumes were duly paid for, and ask him if he would therefore kindly let me have the second one; and without any further payment I should march happily out of the shop with my possession under my arm. Would you not do the same under the same circumstances?

But you *are* under the same circumstances. If you have fulfilled the conditions, you are entitled to two gifts, not just one. You have already taken the one; why not just come and take the other now? Say to the Lord,

Lord, I have complied with the conditions for receiving remission of sins and the gift of the Holy Ghost, but I have foolishly only taken the former. Now at length I have come back to thee to take the gift of the Holy Ghost, and to praise thee for it.

The Diversity of the Experience

But you ask: "How shall I know that the Holy Spirit is come upon me?" I cannot tell *how* you will know, but you *will* know. No description has been given us of the personal sensations and emotions of the disciples at Pentecost. We do not know exactly how they felt, but we do know that their feelings and behavior were somewhat abnormal, because people seeing them said they were intoxicated. When the Holy Spirit falls upon God's people, there will be some things which the world cannot account for. There will be supernatural accompaniments of some kind, though it be no more than an overwhelming sense of the Divine Presence. We cannot and we must not stipulate what particular form such outward expressions will take in any given case, but one thing is sure: that each one upon whom the Spirit of God falls *will unfailingly know it.*

When the Holy Spirit came upon the disciples at Pentecost, there was something quite extraordinary about their behavior, and Peter offered an explanation from God's Word to all who witnessed it. This, in substance, is what he said:

> When the Holy Spirit falls upon believers, some will prophesy, some will dream dreams, and others will see visions. This is what God has stated through the prophet Joel.

But did Peter prophesy? Well, hardly in the sense in which Joel meant it. Did the hundred and twenty prophesy or see visions? We are not told that they did. Did they dream dreams? How could they, for were they not all wide awake? Well then, what did Peter mean by using a quotation that seems scarcely to fit the case at all? In the passage quoted (Joel 2:28–29), prophesy, dreams and visions are said to accompany the outpouring of the Spirit, yet these evidences were apparently lacking at Pentecost.

On the other hand, Joel's prophecy said not a word about "a sound as of the rushing of a mighty wind," nor about "tongues parting asunder like as of fire" as accompaniments of the Spirit's outpouring; yet these were manifest in that upper room. And where in Joel do we find mention of speaking in other tongues? And yet the disciples at Pentecost did so.

What did Peter mean? Imagine him quoting God's Word to show that the experience of Pentecost was the outpouring of the Spirit spoken of by Joel, without a single one of the evidences mentioned by Joel being found at Pentecost. What the Book mentioned, the disciples lacked, and what the disciples had, the Book did not mention! It looks as though

Peter's quotation of the Book disproves his point rather than proving it. What is the explanation of this mystery?

Let us recall that Peter was himself speaking under the control of the Holy Spirit. The Book of the Acts was written by the Spirit's inspiration, and not one word was spoken at random. There is no misfit, but a perfect harmony. Note carefully that Peter did not say: "What you see and hear fulfills what was spoken by the prophet Joel." What he said was: "This is that which hath been spoken by the prophet Joel" (Acts 2:16). It was not a case of fulfillment, but of an experience *of the same order*. "This is that" means that "this which you see and hear is of the same order as that which is foretold." When it is a case of fulfillment, each experience is re-duplicated, and prophecy is prophecy, dreams are dreams, and visions are visions; but when Peter says "This is that," it is not a question of the one being a replica of the other, but of the one belonging to the same category as the other. "This" amounts to the same thing as "that"; "this" is the equivalent of "that"; "this *is* that." What is being emphasized by the Holy Spirit through Peter is the diversity of the experience. The outward evidences may be many and varied, and we have to admit that occasionally they are strange; but the Spirit is one, and he is Lord. (See 1 Corinthians 12:4–6).

What happened to R.A. Torrey[1] when the Holy Spirit came upon him after he had been a minister for years? Let him tell it in his own words:

> I recall the exact spot where I was kneeling in prayer in my study . . . It was a very quiet moment, one of the most quiet moments I ever knew . . . Then God simply said to me, not in any audible voice, but in my heart. "It's yours. Now go and preach." He had already said it to me in his Word in 1 John 5:14–15; but I did not then know my Bible as I know it now, and God had pity on my ignorance and said it directly to my soul . . . I went and preached, and I have been a new minister from

---

[1] Reuben Archer Torrey (1856–1928) was an American evangelist, pastor, educator, and writer. Torrey held evangelistic meetings around the world with song leader Charles Alexander and was called by D. L. Moody to head the Bible Institute of the Chicago Evangelization Society (now Moody Bible Institute), and was the Dean of the Bible Institute of Los Angeles. Torrey, who wrote more than 40 books, is best known for his classics on *How to Pray* and *How to Study the Bible*, which are available in a combined edition in another volume of the Hendrickson Christian Classics series, 2004.

that day to this . . . Some time after this experience (I do not recall just how long after), while sitting in my room one day . . . suddenly . . . I found myself shouting. (I was not brought up to shout and I am not of a shouting temperament, but I shouted like the loudest shouting Methodist.) "Glory to God, glory to God, glory to God," and I could not stop. . . . But that was not when I was baptized with the Holy Spirit. I was baptized with the Holy Spirit when I took him by simple faith in the Word of God.[2]

The outward manifestations in Torrey's case were not the same as those described by Joel or by Peter, but "this is that." It is not a facsimile, yet it is the same thing.

And how did D.L. Moody[3] feel and act when the Spirit came upon him to transform his life and ministry?

I was crying all the time that God would fill me with his Spirit. Well, one day, in the city of New York—oh, what a day!—I cannot describe it, I seldom refer to it; it is almost too sacred an experience to name. Paul had an experience of which he never spoke for fourteen years. I can only say that God revealed himself to me, and I had such an experience of his love that I had to ask him to stay his hand. I went preaching again. The sermons were not different; I did not present any new truths; and yet hundreds were converted. I would not now be placed back where I was before that blessed experience if you should give me all the world—it would be as the small dust of the balance.[4]

The outward manifestation that accompanied Moody's experience did not tally exactly with Joel's description, or Peter's, or Torrey's, but who could doubt that "this" which Moody experienced was "that" experienced by the disciples at Pentecost? It was not the same in manifestation, but it was the very same in essence.

---

[2] *The Holy Spirit, Who He Is and What He Does*, by R.A. Torrey, D.D., pp. 198–9. [1927, London: Fleming H. Revell.]

[3] Dwight Lyman Moody (1837–1899) is one of the late nineteenth century's best known Christians. Over his 40 year career, he founded the Northfield Schools in Massachusetts, Moody Church and Moody Bible Institute in Chicago, and the Colportage Association; converted hundreds of thousands of people to Christianity; founded a major Christian publishing business; and inspired many preachers to conduct revivals.

[4] *The Life of Dwight L. Moody*, by his son, W.R. Moody, p. 149. [1900, New York: Fleming H. Revell Co.]

And what was the experience of the great Charles Finney[5] when the power of the Holy Ghost came upon him?

> I received a mighty baptism of the Holy Ghost without any expectation of it, without ever having the thought in my mind that there was any such thing for me, without any recollection that I had ever heard the thing mentioned by any person in the world, the Holy Spirit descended upon me in a manner that seemed to go through me body and soul. No words can express the wonderful love that was shed abroad in my heart. I wept aloud with joy and love.[6]

Finney's experience was not a duplicate of Pentecost, nor of Torrey's experience, nor of Moody's; but "this" certainly was "that."

When the Holy Spirit is poured out upon God's people, their experiences will differ widely. Some will receive new vision, others will know a new liberty in soul-winning, others will proclaim the Word of God with fresh power, and yet others will be filled with heavenly joy or overflowing praise. "This . . . and this . . . and this . . . is that!" Let us praise the Lord for every new experience that relates to the exaltation of Christ and of which it can truly be said that "this" is an evidence of "that." There is nothing stereotyped about God's dealings with his children. Therefore we must not by our prejudices and preconceptions make water-tight compartments for the working of his Spirit, either in our own lives or in the lives of others. This applies equally to those who require some particular manifestation (such as "speaking with tongues") as evidence that the spirit has come upon them and to those who deny that any manifestation is given at all. We must leave God free to work as he wills, and to give what evidence he pleases of the work he does. He is Lord, and it is not for us to legislate for him.

---

[5] Charles Grandison Finney (1792–1875), American evangelist, helped spark the Second Great Awakening in the late 1800s. Finney was born in Warren, Connecticut, but soon after his family moved to the western frontier, and Finney's ministry was marked by pioneer spirit. Trained as a lawyer and committed to the full authority of the Bible, Finney was extravagant, controversial, and effective in his revivalist preaching, meetings, and writing. He is best known for his *Revival Lectures.*

[6] *Autobiography of Charles G. Finney,* chapter 2. [1908, Westwood, N. J.: Fleming H. Revell. Originally published as *Memoirs of Rev. Charles G. Finney,* 1903.]

Let us rejoice that Jesus is on the throne, and let us praise him that, since he has been glorified, the Spirit has been poured out upon us all. As we behold him there and accept the divine fact in all the simplicity of faith, we shall know it with such assurance in our own hearts that we shall dare to proclaim with confidence—"This is that!"

The Spirit Indwelling

We move on now to the second aspect of the gift of the Holy Spirit, which, as we shall see in our next chapter, is more particularly the subject of Romans 8. It is that which we have spoken of as the Spirit indwelling. "If so, be that the Spirit of God dwelleth in you . . . " (Romans 8:9). "If the Spirit of him that raised up Jesus from the dead dwelleth in you . . ." (Rom 8:11).

As with the Spirit outpoured, so with the Spirit indwelling; if we are to know in experience that which is ours in fact, our first need is of divine revelation. When we see Christ as Lord objectively—that is, as exalted to the throne in Heaven—then we shall experience the power of the Spirit upon us. When we see Christ as Lord subjectively—that is, as effective Ruler within our lives—then we shall know the power of the Spirit within us.

A revelation of the indwelling Spirit was the remedy Paul offered the Corinthian Christians for their unspirituality. It is important to note that the Christians in Corinth had become preoccupied with the visible signs of the Holy Spirit's outpouring and were making much of "tongues" and miracles, while at the same time their lives were full of contradictions and were a reproach to the Lord's Name. They had quite evidently received the Holy Spirit, and yet they remained spiritually immature; and the remedy God offered them for this, is the remedy he offers his Church today for the same complaint.

In his letter to them Paul wrote: *"Know ye not that ye are a temple of God, and that the Spirit of God dwelleth in you?"* (1 Corinthians 3:16) For others he prayed for enlightenment of heart, *". . . that ye may know"* (Ephesians 1:18). A knowledge of divine facts was the need of the Christians then, and it is no less the need of Christians today. We need the eyes of our understanding opened to know that God himself, through the Holy

Spirit, has taken up his abode in our hearts. In the person of the Spirit, God is present, and Christ is no less truly present too. Thus, if the Holy Spirit dwells in our hearts, we have the Father and the Son abiding in us. That is no mere theory or doctrine, but a blessed reality. We may perhaps have realized that the Spirit is actually within our hearts, but have we realized that he is a Person? Have we understood that to have the Spirit within us, is it to have the living God within?

To many Christians the Holy Spirit is quite unreal. They regard him as a mere influence—and influence for good, no doubt, but just an influence for all that. In their thinking, conscience and the Spirit are more or less identified as some "thing" within them that brings them to book when they are bad and tries to show them how to be good. The trouble with the Corinthian Christians was not that they lacked the indwelling Spirit, but that they lacked the knowledge of his presence. They failed to realize the greatness of the One who had come to make his abode in their hearts; so Paul wrote to them: "Know ye not that ye are a temple of God, and that the Spirit of God dwelleth in you?" Yes, that was the remedy for their unspirituality—just to know who He really was, who dwelt within.

The Treasure In the Vessel

Do you know, my friends, that the Spirit within you is very God? Oh, that our eyes were opened to see the greatness of God's gift! Oh, that we might realize the vastness of the resources secreted in our own hearts! I could shout with joy as I think, "The Spirit who dwells within me is no mere influence, but a living Person; he is very God. The infinite God is within my heart!" I am at a loss to convey to you the blessedness of this discovery, that the Holy Spirit dwelling within my heart is a Person. I can only repeat: "He is a Person!" and repeat it again: "He is a Person!" and repeat it yet again: "He is a Person!" Oh, my friends, I would fain repeat it to you a hundred times—*The Spirit of God within me is a Person!* I am only an earthen vessel, but in that earthen vessel I carry a treasure of unspeakable worth, even the Lord of glory.

All the worry and fret of God's children would end if their eyes were opened to see the greatness of the treasure hid in their hearts. Do you know, there are resources enough in your own heart to meet the demand of every circumstance in which you will ever find yourself? Do you know there is power enough there to move the city in which you live? Do you know there is power enough to shake the universe? Let me tell you once more—I say it with the utmost reverence: You who have been born again of the Spirit of God—you carry God in your heart!

All the flippancy of the children of God would cease too if they realized the greatness of the treasure deposited within them. If you have only ten shillings in your pocket, you can march gaily along the street, talking lightly as you go, and swinging your stick in the air. It matters little if you lose your money, for there is not much at stake. But if you carry a thousand pounds in your pocket, the position is vastly different, and your whole demeanor will be different too. There will be great gladness in your heart, but no careless jaunting along the road; and once in a while you will slacken your pace and, slipping your hand into your pocket, you will quietly finger your treasure again, and then with joyful solemnity continue on your way.

In Old Testament times there were hundreds of tents in the camp of Israel, but there was one tent quite different from all the rest. In the common tents you could do just as you pleased—eat or fast, work or rest, be joyful or sober, noisy or silent. But that other tent was a tent that commanded reverence and awe. You might move in and out of the common tents talking noisily and laughing gaily, but as soon as you neared that special tent you instinctively walked more quietly, and when you stood right before it you bowed your head in solemn silence. No one could touch it with impunity. If man or beast dared to do so, death was the sure penalty. What was so very special about it? *It was the temple of the living God.* There was little unusual about the tent itself, for it was outwardly of very ordinary material, but the great God had chosen to make it his abode.

Do you realize what happened at your conversion? God came into your heart and made it his temple. In Solomon's days God dwelt in a temple made of stone; today he dwells in a temple composed of living believers. When we really see that God has made our hearts his dwelling place, what a deep reverence will come over our lives! All lightness, all frivolity will end, and all self-pleasing too, when we *know* that we are the temple of God and that the Spirit of God dwells within us. Has it really come home to you that wherever you go, you carry with you the Holy Spirit of God? You do not just carry your Bible with you, or even much good teaching about God, but God himself.

The reason why many Christians do not experience the power of the Spirit, though he actually dwells in their hearts, is that they lack reverence. And they lack reverence because they have not had their eyes opened to the fact of his presence. The fact is there, but they have not seen it. Why is it that some Christians are living victorious lives while others live in a state of constant defeat? The difference is not accounted for by the presence or absence of the Spirit (for he dwells in the heart of every child of God) but by this, that some recognize his indwelling and others do not. True revelation of the fact of the Spirit's indwelling will revolutionize the life of any Christian.

The Absolute Lordship of Christ

> Know ye not that your body is a temple of the Holy Ghost which is in you, which ye have from God? And ye are not your own; for ye were bought with a price: glorify God therefore in your body (1 Cor. 6:19–20).

This verse now takes us a stage further, for, when once we have made the discovery of the fact that we are the dwelling place of God, then a full surrender of ourselves to God must follow. When we see that we are the temple of God, we shall immediately acknowledge that we are not our own. Consecration will follow revelation. The difference between victorious Christians and defeated ones is not that some have the Spirit while others have not, but that some *know* his indwelling and others do not, and that consequently some recognize the divine ownership of their lives while others are still their own masters.

Revelation is the first step to holiness, and consecration is the second. A day must come in our lives, as definite as the day of our conversion, when we give up all right to ourselves and submit to the absolute Lordship of Jesus Christ. There may be a practical issue raised by God to test the reality of our consecration, but whether that be so or not, there must be a day when, without reservation, we surrender everything to him—ourselves, our families, our possessions, our business and our time. All we are and have becomes his, to be held henceforth entirely at his disposal. From that day we are no longer our own masters, but only stewards. Not until the Lordship of Christ is a settled thing in our hearts can the Spirit really operate effectively in us. He cannot direct our lives effectually until all control of them is committed to him. If we do not give him absolute authority in our lives, he can be present, but he cannot be powerful. The power of the Spirit is stayed.

Are you living for the Lord, or for yourself? Perhaps that is too general a question, so let me be more specific. Is there anything God is asking of you that you are withholding from him? Is there any point of contention between you and him? Not till every controversy is settled and the Holy Spirit is given his full place can he reproduce the life of Christ in any believer.

An American friend, now with the Lord, whose name we will call Paul, cherished the hope from his early youth that one day he would be called "Dr. Paul." When he was quite a little chap he began to dream of the day when he would enter the university, and he imagined himself first studying for his M.A. degree and then for his Ph.D. Then at length the glad day would arrive when all would greet him as "Dr. Paul."

The Lord saved him and called him to preach, and before long he became pastor of a large congregation. By that time he had his degree and was studying for his doctorate, but, despite splendid progress in his studies and a good measure of success as a pastor, he was a very dissatisfied man. He was a Christian minister, but his life was not Christ-like; he had the Spirit of God within him, but he did not enjoy the Spirit's presence or experience his power. He thought to himself,

> I am a preacher of the Gospel and the pastor of a church. I tell my people they should love the Word of God, but I do not really love it myself. I exhort them to pray, but I myself have little inclination to pray. I tell them to live a holy life, but my own life is not holy. I warn them not to love the world, and, though outwardly I shun it, yet in my heart I myself still love it dearly.

In his distress he cried to the Lord to cause him to know the power of the indwelling Spirit, but though he prayed and prayed for months, no answer came. Then he fasted and besought the Lord to show him any hindrance there might be in his life. That answer was not long in coming, and it was this:

> I long that you should know the power of my Spirit, but your heart is set on something that I do not wish you to have. You have yielded to me all but one thing, and that one thing you are holding to yourself—your Ph.D.

Well, to you or me it might be of little consequence whether we were addressed as plain "Mr. Paul" or as "Dr. Paul," but to him it was his very life. He had dreamed of it from childhood and labored for it all through his youth, and now the thing he prized above all was almost within his grasp. In two short months it would be his.

So he reasoned with the Lord in this wise:

> Is there any harm for me to be a Doctor of Philosophy? Will it not bring much more glory to thy Name to have a Dr. Paul preaching the Gospel than a plain Mr. Paul?

But God does not change his mind, and all Mr. Paul's sound reasoning did not alter the Lord's word to him. Every time he prayed about the matter, he got the same answer. Then, reasoning having failed, he resorted to bargaining with the Lord. He promised to go here or there, to do this or that, if only the Lord would allow him to have his doctor's degree; but still the Lord did not change. And all the while Mr. Paul was becoming more and more hungry to know the fullness of the Spirit. This state of affairs continued to within two days of his final examination.

It was Saturday, and Mr. Paul settled down to prepare his sermon for the following day, but, study as he would, he could get no message. The ambition of a lifetime was just within reach of realization, but God made it clear that he must choose between the power he could sway through a doctor's degree and the power of God's Spirit swaying his life. That evening he yielded. "Lord," he said, "I am willing to be plain Mr. Paul all my days, but I want to know the power of the Holy Ghost in my life."

He rose from his knees and wrote a letter to his examiners, asking to be excused from the examination on the Monday, and giving his reason. Then he retired, very happy, but not conscious of any unusual experience.

Next morning he told his congregation that for the first time in six years he had no sermon to preach, and explained how it came about. The Lord blessed that testimony more abundantly than any of his well-prepared sermons, and from that time God owned him in an altogether new way. From that day he knew separation from the world, no longer as an outward thing but as a deep inward reality, and as a result, the blessedness of the Spirit's presence and power became his daily experience.

God is waiting for a settlement of all our controversies with him. With Mr. Paul it was a question of his doctor's degree, but with us it may be something quite different. Our complete surrender of ourselves to the Lord generally hinges upon some one particular thing, and God waits for that one thing. He must have it, for he must have our all. I was greatly impressed by something a great national leader wrote in his autobiography: "I want nothing for myself; I want everything for my country." If a man can be willing that his country should have everything and he himself nothing, cannot we say to our God: "Lord, I want nothing for myself; I want all for thee. I will what *thou* willest, and I want to have nothing outside thy will." Not until we take the place of a servant can he take his place as Lord. He is not calling us to devote ourselves to his cause: he is asking us to yield ourselves unconditionally to his will. Are you prepared for that?

Another friend of mine, like my friend Mr. Paul, had a controversy with the Lord. Before his conversion he fell in love, and as soon as he was saved he sought to win the one he loved to Christ, but she would have nothing to do with spiritual things. The Lord made it clear to him that his relations with that girl must be broken off, but he was deeply devoted to her, so he evaded the issue, while continuing as before to serve the Lord and to win souls for him. But he became conscious of his need for holiness, and that consciousness marked for him the beginning of dark days. He asked for the Spirit's fullness that he might have power to live a holy life, but God seemed continually to ignore his request.

One morning he had to preach in another city and he spoke from Psalm 73:25: "Whom have I in heaven but thee? And there is none upon earth that I desire beside thee." On his return home he went to a prayer meeting, and there a sister got up and read the very same verse from which, unknown to her, he had just preached, and followed it with the question: "Can we truly say: 'There is none upon earth that I desire beside thee'?" There was power in that word. It struck right home to his heart, and he had to admit to himself that he could not truthfully say that he desired no one in Heaven or earth apart from his Lord. He saw, there and then, that, for him, everything hinged upon his willingness to give up the girl he loved.

For some, perhaps, it might not have involved much, but for him it was everything. So he began to reason with the Lord: "Lord, I will go to Tibet and work for thee there if I may marry that girl." But the Lord seemed to care a great deal more about his relationship with that girl than about his going to Tibet, and no amount of reasoning on his part availed to effect any change of emphasis on the part of the Lord. The controversy went on for several months, and whenever the young man pleaded for the fullness of the Spirit, God still pointed to the same thing. But a day came when His grace triumphed, and that young man looked up to Him and acknowledged: "Lord, I can truly now say, 'There is none upon earth that I desire beside thee.'" It was the dawn of a new day for him.

A forgiven sinner is quite different from an ordinary sinner, and a consecrated Christian is quite different from an ordinary Christian. May the Lord bring us to a definite issue regarding the question of his Lordship. If we yield wholly to him and claim the power of the indwelling Spirit, we need wait for no special feelings or supernatural manifestations, but can simply look up and praise him that something has already happened. We can confidently thank him that the glory of God has already filled his temple. "Know ye not that your body is a temple of the Holy Ghost which is in you, *which ye have from God?*"[7]

---

[7] 1 Cor. 6:19

CHAPTER 9

The Meaning and Value of Romans Seven

We must return now to Romans. We broke off at the end of chapter 6 in order to consider two related subjects, namely, God's eternal purpose, which is the motive and goal of our walk with him; and the Holy Spirit, who supplies the power and resource to bring us to that goal. We come now to Romans 7, a chapter which many have felt to be almost superfluous. Perhaps indeed it would be so if Christians really saw that the old creation has been ruled out by the Cross of Christ, and an entirely new creation brought in by his resurrection. If we have come to the point where we really "know" that, and "reckon" on that, and "present ourselves" on the basis of that, then *perhaps* we have no need of Romans 7.

Others have felt that the chapter is in the wrong place. They would have put it between the fifth and sixth chapters. After chapter 6, all is so perfect, so straightforward; and then comes this astonishing breakdown and the cry, "O wretched man that I am!" Could anything be more of an anticlimax? And so some have argued that Paul is speaking here of his unregenerate experience and of his failure, as a Jew, to keep the Law. Well, we must admit that some of what he describes here is not a *Christian* experience, but none the less many Christians do experience it. What then, is the teaching of this chapter?

Romans 6 deals with freedom from sin. Romans 7 deals with freedom from the Law. In chapter 6 Paul has told us how we could be delivered from sin, and we concluded that this was all that was required. Chapter 7 now teaches that deliverance from sin is not enough, but that we also need to know deliverance from the Law. If we are not fully emancipated from the Law, we can never know full emancipation from sin. But what is the difference between deliverance from sin and deliverance from the Law? We all see the value of the former, but where, we wonder, is the need for the latter? For answer, we must first of all ask our selves what the Law is, and what is its special value for us.

The Flesh and Man's Breakdown

Romans 7 has a new lesson to teach us. It is found in the discovery that I am "in the flesh" (Rom. 7:5), that "I am carnal" (7:14), and that "in me, that is, in my flesh, dwelleth no good thing" (7:18). This goes beyond the question of sin, for it relates also the matter of pleasing God. We are dealing here not with sin in its forms, but with man in his carnal state. The latter includes the former, but it takes us a stage further, for it leads to the discovery that in this realm too we are totally impotent, and that "they that are in the flesh cannot please God" (Rom. 8:8). How then is this discovery made? It is made with the help of the Law.

Let us retrace our steps for a minute and attempt to describe what is probably the experience of many. Many a Christian is truly saved, and yet bound by sin. It is not that he is necessarily living under the power of sin all the time, but that there are certain particular sins hampering him continually so that he commits them over and over again. One day he hears the full message of the Gospel, that the Lord Jesus not only died to cleanse away our sins, but that when he died, he included us sinners in his death; so that not only were our sins dealt with, but we ourselves were dealt with too. The man's eyes are opened, and he *knows* he has been crucified with Christ. Two things follow that revelation. In the first place he *reckons* that he has died and risen with his Lord. In the second place, recognizing God's claim upon him, and that he has no more right over himself, he *presents himself* to God as alive from the dead. This is the commencement of a beautiful Christian life, full of praise to the Lord.

But then he begins to reason as follows:

> I have died with Christ and am raised with him, and I have given myself over to him forever; now I must do something for him, since he has done so much for me. I want to please him and do his will.

So, after the step of consecration, he seeks to discover the will of God, and sets himself to carry it out. Then he makes a strange discovery. He thought he could do the will of God, because he thought he loved it, but gradually he finds he does not always like it at all. At times he even finds a distinct reluctance to pursue it, and often when he tries to put it into practice, he finds he cannot. Then he begins to question his experience. He asks himself:

> Did I really know? Yes! Did I really reckon? Yes! Did I really give myself to him? Yes! Have I withdrawn my consecration? No! Then whatever is the matter now?

For the more this man tries to do the will of God, the more he fails. Ultimately he comes to the conclusion that he never really loved God's will at all, so he prays for the desire as well as the power to do it. He confesses his disobedience and promises never to disobey again. But scarcely has he got up from his knees when he falls once more; before he reaches the point of victory, he is conscious of defeat. Then he says to himself: "Perhaps my last decision was not definite enough. This time I will be absolutely definite." So he brings all his will-power to bear on the situation, only to find greater defeat than ever awaiting him the next time a choice has to be made. Then at last he echoes the words of Paul:

> For I know that in me, that is, in my flesh, dwelleth no good thing: for to will is present with me, but to do that which is good is not. For the good which I would I do not: but the evil which I would not, that I practice (Rom. 7:18–19).

He has reached the point of desperation.

What the Law Teaches

Many Christians find themselves suddenly launched into the experience of Romans 7, and they do not understand why. They fancy Romans 6 is quite enough. Having grasped that, they think there can be no more question of failure, and then to their utmost surprise they find themselves in the midst Romans 7. What is the explanation?

First, let us be quite clear that the death with Christ described in Romans 6 is fully adequate to cover all our needs. It is the *explanation* of that death, with all that follows from it in chapter 6, that is as yet incomplete. We are as yet still in ignorance of the truth set forth in chapter 7. Romans 7 is given to us to explain and make real the statement in Romans 6:14, that: "Sin shall not have dominion over you: for ye are not under law, but under grace." The trouble is that we do not yet know deliverance from law. What, then, is the meaning of Law?

Grace means that God does something for me; law means that I do something for God. God has certain holy and righteous demands which he places upon me: that is law. Now if law means that God requires something of me for their fulfillment, then deliverance from law means that he no longer requires that from me, but himself provides it. Law implies that God requires me to do something *for him;* deliverance from law implies that he *exempts me* from doing it, and that in grace he does it himself. *I* (where "I" is the "carnal" man of ch. 7:14) *need do nothing for God:* that is deliverance from law. The trouble in Romans 7 is that man in the flesh tried to do something for God. As soon as you try to please God in that way, then you place yourself under Law, and the experience of Romans 7 begins to be yours.

As we seek to understand this, let it be settled at the outset that the fault does not lie with the Law. Paul says, "the law is holy, and the commandment holy, and righteous, and good" (Rom. 7:12). No, there is nothing wrong with the Law, but there is something decidedly wrong with me. The demands of the Law are righteous, but the person upon whom the demands are made, is unrighteous. The trouble is not that the Law's demands are unjust, but that I am unable to meet them. It may be all right for the government to require payment of £100, but it will be all wrong if I have only ten shillings with which to meet the payment!

I am a man "sold under sin" (Rom. 7:14). Sin has dominion over me. True, as long as you leave me alone, I seem to be rather a fine type of man. It is when you ask me to *do* something that my sinfulness comes to light.

If you have a very clumsy servant, and he just sits still and does nothing, then his clumsiness does not appear. If he does nothing all day he will be of little use to you, it is true, but at least he will do no damage that way. But if you say to him: "Now come along, don't idle away your time; get up and do something," then immediately the trouble begins. He knocks the chair over as he gets up, stumbles over a footstool a few paces further on, then smashes some precious dish as soon as he handles it. If you make no demands upon him, his clumsiness is never noticed, but as soon as you ask him to do anything, his awkwardness is apparent at once. The demands were all right, but the man was all wrong. He was as clumsy a man when he was sitting still as when he was working, but it was your demands that made manifest the clumsiness which, whether he was active or inactive, was all the time in his make-up.

We are all sinners by nature. If God asks nothing of us, all seems to go well, but as soon as he demands something of us, the occasion is provided for a grand display of our sinfulness. The Law makes our weakness manifest. While you let me sit still, I appear to be all right, but when you ask me to do anything I am sure to spoil it, and if you trust me with a second thing I will as surely spoil that also. When a holy law is applied to a sinful man, then his sinfulness comes out in full display.

God knows who I am; he knows that from head to foot I am full of sin; he knows that I am weakness incarnate; that I can do nothing. The trouble is that I do not know it. I admit that all men are sinners and that therefore I am a sinner; but I imagine that I am not such a hopeless sinner as some. God must bring us all to the place where we see that we are utterly weak and helpless. While we say so, we do not wholly believe it, and God has to do something to convince us of the fact. Had it not been for the Law, we should never have known how weak we are. Paul had reached that point. He makes this clear when he says in Romans 7:7, "I had not known sin, except through the law: for I had not known coveting, except the law had said, 'Thou shalt not covet.'" Whatever might be his experience with the rest of the Law, it was the tenth commandment, which literally translated is: "Thou shalt not desire . . . " that found him out. There his incapacity stared him in the face!

The more we try to keep the Law, the more our weakness is manifest and the deeper we get into Romans 7, until it is clearly demonstrated to us that we are hopelessly weak. God knew it all along, but we did not, and so God had to bring us through painful experiences to a recognition of the fact. We need to have our weakness proved to ourselves beyond dispute. That is why God gave us the Law.

So we can say, reverently, that God never gave us the Law to keep; he gave us the Law to break! He well knew that we could not keep it. We are so bad that he asks no favor and makes no demands. Never has any man succeeded in making himself acceptable to God by means of the Law. Nowhere in the New Testament are men of faith told that they are to keep the Law; but it does say that the Law was given so that there should be transgression. "The law came in . . . that the trespass might abound" (Rom. 5:20). The Law was given to make us law-breakers! No doubt I am a sinner in Adam;

> Howbeit, I had not know sin, except through the law: . . . for apart from the law sin is dead . . . but when the commandment came, sin revived, and I died (Rom. 7:7–9).

The Law is that which exposes our true nature. Alas, we are so conceited, and think ourselves so strong, that God has to give us something to test us and prove how weak we are. At last we see it, and confess: "I am a sinner through and through, and of myself I can do nothing whatever to please a holy God."

No, the Law was not given in the expectation that we would keep it. It was given in the full knowledge that we would break it; and when we have broken it so completely as to be convinced of our utter need, then the Law has served its purpose. It has been our schoolmaster to bring us to Christ, that in us He may himself fulfill it (Gal. 3:24).

Christ the End of the Law

In Romans 6 we saw how God delivered us from sin; in Romans 7 we see how he delivers us from the Law. Chapter 6 shows us the way of deliverance from sin in the picture of a master and his slave; chapter 7 shows us the way of deliverance from the Law in the picture of two husbands and a wife. The relation between sin and the sinner is that of master to slave; the relation between the Law and the sinner is that of husband to wife.

Notice first that, in the picture by which, in Romans 7:1–4, Paul illustrates our deliverance from the Law, there is only one woman, while there are two husbands.[1] The woman is in a very difficult position, for she can only be wife of one of the two, and unfortunately she is married to the less desirable one. Let us make no mistake; the man to whom she is married is a good man; but the trouble lies here, that the husband and wife are totally unsuited to one another. He is a most particular man, accurate to a degree; she on the other hand is decidedly easy-going. With him all is definite and precise; with her all is casual and haphazard. He wants everything just so, while she takes things as they come. How could there be happiness in such a home?

And then that husband is so exacting! He is always making demands upon her. And yet one cannot find fault with him, for as a husband he has a right to expect something of his wife; and besides, all his demands are perfectly legitimate. There is nothing wrong with the man and nothing wrong with his demands; the trouble is that he has the wrong kind of wife to carry them out. The two cannot get on at all; theirs are utterly incompatible natures. Thus the poor woman is in great distress. She is fully aware that she often makes mistakes, but living with such a husband it seems as though *everything* she says and does is wrong! What hope is there

---

[1] Romans 7:1-10 (KJV): ¹Know ye not, brethren, (for I speak to them that know the law,) how that the law hath dominion over a man as long as he liveth? ²For the woman which hath an husband is bound by the law to her husband so long as he liveth; but if the husband be dead, she is loosed from the law of her husband. ³So then if, while her husband liveth, she be married to another man, she shall be called an adulteress: but if her husband be dead, she is free from that law; so that she is no adulteress, though she be married to another man. ⁴Wherefore, my brethren, ye also are become dead to the law by the body of Christ; that ye should be married to another, even to him who is raised from the dead, that we should bring forth fruit unto God. ⁵For when we were in the flesh, the motions of sins, which were by the law, did work in our members to bring forth fruit unto death. ⁶But now we are delivered from the law, that being dead wherein we were held; that we should serve in newness of spirit, and not in the oldness of the letter. ⁷What shall we say then? Is the law sin? God forbid. Nay, I had not known sin, but by the law: for I had not known lust, except the law had said, "Thou shalt not covet." ⁸But sin, taking occasion by the commandment, wrought in me all manner of concupiscence. For without the law sin was dead. ⁹For I was alive without the law once: but when the commandment came, sin revived, and I died. ¹⁰And the commandment, which was ordained to life, I found to be unto death.

for her? If only she were married to that other Man, all would be well. He is no less exacting than her husband, but he also helps much. She would fain marry him, but her husband is still alive. What can she do? She is "bound by law to the husband" and unless he dies, she cannot legitimately marry that other Man.

This picture is not drawn by me but by the apostle Paul. The first husband is the Law; the second husband is Christ; and you are the woman. The Law requires much, but offers no help in the carrying out of its requirements. The Lord Jesus requires just as much, yea more (Matt. 5:21–48) but what he requires from us, he himself carries out in us. The Law makes demands and leaves us helpless to fulfill them; Christ makes demands, but he himself fulfills in us the very demands he makes. Little wonder that the woman desires to be freed from the first husband that she may marry that other Man! But her only hope of release is through the death of her first husband, and he holds on to life most tenaciously. Indeed, there is not the least prospect of his passing away. "Till heaven and earth pass away, one jot or one tittle shall in no wise pass away from the law, till all things be accomplished (Matt. 5:18).

The Law is going to continue for all eternity. If the Law will never pass away, then how can I ever be united to Christ? How can I marry a second husband if my first husband resolutely refuses to die? There is one way out. If *he* will not die, *I* can die, and if I die the marriage relationship is dissolved. And that is exactly God's way of deliverance from the Law. The most important point to note in this section of Romans 7 is the transition from verse 3 to verse 4. Verses 1 to 3 show that the husband should die, but in verse 4 we see that in fact it is the woman who dies. The Law does not pass away, but I pass away, and by death I am freed from the Law. Let us realize clearly that the Law can never pass away. *God's righteous demands remain forever,* and if I live, I must meet those demands; but if I die, the Law has lost its claim upon me. It cannot follow me beyond the grave.

Thus exactly the same principle operates in our deliverance from the Law as in our deliverance from sin. When I have died, my old master, Sin, still continues to live, but his power over his slave extends as far as the grave and no further. He could ask me to do a hundred and one things when I was alive, but when I am dead, he calls on me in vain. I am forever freed from his tyranny. So it is with regard to the Law. While the woman lives, she is bound to her husband, but with her death the marriage bond is dissolved and she is "discharged from the law of her husband." The Law may still make demands, but for me, its power to enforce them is ended.

Now the vital question arises: "How do I die?" And the preciousness of our Lord's work comes in just here: "Ye also were made dead to the law through the body of Christ." (Rom. 7:4). When Christ died, his body was broken, and since God placed me in him (1 Cor. 1:30), I have been broken too. When he was crucified, I was crucified with him. In the sight of God, his death included mine. On the hill of Calvary, it was forever done.

"Wherefore, my brethren, ye also were made dead to the law" (Rom. 7:4). That woman's husband may be very well and strong, but if she dies, he may make as many demands upon her as he likes; it will not affect her in the slightest. Death has released her free from all his claims. The all-inclusive death of Jesus Christ has forever freed us from the Law.

But that is not all. Remember, our Lord did not remain in the grave. On the third day he rose again; and since we are still in him we are risen too. The body of the Lord Jesus speaks not only of his death but of his resurrection, for his resurrection was a bodily resurrection. Thus "through the body of Christ" we are not only "dead to the law" but alive unto God.

God's purpose in uniting us to Christ was not merely negative; it was gloriously positive—"that ye should be joined to another" (Rom. 7:4). Death has dissolved the old marriage relationship, so that the woman, driven to despair by the constant demands of her former husband, who never lifted a little finger to help her carry them out, is now set free to marry the other Man, who with every demand he makes becomes in her the power for its fulfillment.

And what is the issue of this new union? "That we might bring forth fruit unto God" (Rom. 7:4). By the body of Christ that foolish, sinful woman has died, but being united to him in death she is united to him also in resurrection, and in the power of that resurrection life, hers becomes a fruitful life. The life of the risen Lord in her empowers her for all the claims God's holiness makes upon her. The Law of God is not annulled; it is perfectly fulfilled, for the risen Lord now lives out his life in her, and his life is always well-pleasing to the Father.

What is the most obvious thing that happens when a woman marries? She changes her name. She no longer bears her own name but that of her husband; and she shares not his name only but his possessions also. Every thing that belongs to him, belongs now equally to her. All of a sudden she is amazingly enriched. And so it is when we are joined to Christ. All that is His becomes ours, and with his infinite resources at our disposal, we need never again fear that we shall be unable to meet all his demands.

Our End Is God's Beginning

Now that we have settled the doctrinal side of the question we must come down to practical issues, staying a little longer with the negative aspect and keeping the positive for our next chapter. What does it mean in everyday life to be delivered from the Law? At the risk of a little overstatement, I reply, "It means that from henceforth I am going to do nothing whatever for God: I am never again going to try to please Him."

"What a doctrine!" you exclaim. "What awful heresy! You cannot possibly mean that!"

But remember, if I try to please God "in the flesh," then immediately I place myself under the Law. I broke the Law; the Law pronounced the death sentence; the sentence was executed, and now by death I—the carnal "I" (Rom. 7:14)—have been set free from all its claims. There is still a Law of God, and now there is in fact a "new commandment" that is infinitely more exacting than the old, but, Praise God! its demands are being met, for it is Christ who now fulfills them; it is Christ who works in me what is well-pleasing to God. "I came . . . to fulfill [the law]" were his words (Matt. 5:17). Thus it is that Paul, from the ground of resurrection, can say:

> Work out your own salvation with fear and trembling; for it is God which worketh in you both to will and to work, for his good pleasure (Phil. 2:12–13).

It is God that worketh in you. Deliverance from law does not mean that we are free from doing the will of God. It certainly does not mean that we are going to be lawless. Very much the reverse! What it does mean however is that we are free from doing that will *as of ourselves*. Being fully persuaded that we cannot do it, we cease trying to please God *from the ground of the old man.* Having at last reached the point of utter despair in ourselves so that we cease even to try, we put our trust in the Lord to manifest his resurrection life in us.

Let me illustrate by what I have seen in my own country. In China most bearers can carry a load of salt weighing 120 kilos, a few even as much as 250 kilos. Now along comes a man who can carry only 120 kilos, and here is a load of 250 kilos. He knows perfectly well he cannot carry it, and if he is wise he will say: "I won't touch it!" But the temptation to try is ingrained in human nature, so although he cannot possibly carry it, nevertheless, he has a go. As a youngster I used to amuse myself watching ten or twenty of these fellows come along and try, though every one of them knew he could not possibly manage it. In the end he must give up and make way for the man who could.

The sooner we too give up trying the better, for if we monopolize the task, there is no room for the Holy Spirit. But if we say: "I'll not do it; I'll trust thee to do it for me," then we shall find that a Power stronger than ourselves is carrying us through.

In 1923 I met a famous Canadian evangelist. I had said in an address something along the above lines, and as we walked back to his home afterwards he remarked: "The note of Romans 7 is seldom sounded nowadays; it is good to hear it again. The day I was delivered from the Law was a day of Heaven on earth. After being a Christian for years I was still trying my best to please God, but the more I tried the more I failed. I regarded God as the greatest Demander in the universe, but I found myself impotent to fulfill the least of his demands. Suddenly one day, as I read Romans 7, light dawned and I saw that I had not only been delivered from sin but from the Law as well. In my amazement I jumped up and said: "Lord, are you really making no demands on me? Then I need do nothing more for You!"

God's requirements have not altered, but we are not the ones to meet them. Praise God, he is the Lawgiver on the Throne, and he is the Lawkeeper in my heart. He who gave the Law, himself keeps it. He makes the demands, but he also meets them. My friend could well jump up and shout when he found he had nothing to do, and all who make a like discovery can do the same. As long as we are trying to do anything, he can do nothing. It is because of our trying that we fail and fail and fail. God wants to demonstrate to us that we can do nothing at all, and until that is fully recognized our despair and disillusion will never cease.

A brother who was trying to struggle into victory remarked to me one day, "I do not know why I am so weak."

"The trouble with you," I said, "is that you are weak enough not to do the will of God, but you are not weak enough to keep out of things altogether. You are still not weak enough. When you are reduced to utter weakness and are persuaded that you can do nothing whatever, then God will do everything." We all need to come to the point where we say: "Lord, I am unable to do anything for thee, but I trust thee to do everything in me."

I was once staying in a place in China with some twenty other brothers. There was inadequate provision for bathing in the home where we stayed, so we went for a daily plunge in the river. On one occasion a brother had cramp in one leg, and I suddenly saw he was sinking fast, so I motioned to another brother, who was an expert swimmer, to hasten to his rescue. But to my astonishment he made no move. So I grew desperate and called out: "Don't you see the man is drowning?" and the other brothers, about as agitated as I was, shouted vigorously too. But our good swimmer still did not move. Calm and collected, he remained just where he was, apparently postponing the unwelcome task. Meantime the voice of the poor drowning brother grew fainter and his efforts feebler. In my heart I said: "I hate that man! Think of his letting a brother drown before his very eyes and not going to the rescue!"

But when the man was actually sinking, with a few swift strokes the swimmer was at his side, and both were soon safely ashore. Nevertheless, when I got an opportunity, I aired my views. "I have never seen any Christian who loved his life quite as much as you do," I said. "Think of the distress you would have saved that brother if you had considered yourself a little less and him a little more." But the swimmer, I soon discovered, knew his business better than I did. "Had I gone earlier," he said, "he would have clutched me so fast that both of us would have gone under. A drowning man cannot be saved until he is utterly exhausted and ceases to make the slightest effort to save himself."

Do you see the point? When *we* give up the case, then *God* will take it up. He is waiting until we are at an end of our resources and can do nothing more for ourselves. God has condemned all that is of the old creation and consigned it to the Cross. The flesh profits *nothing*! If we try to do anything in the flesh we are virtually repudiating the Cross of Christ. God has declared it to be fit only for death. If we truly believe that, then we confirm God's verdict by abandoning all fleshly efforts to please him. For our every attempt to do his will is a denial of his declaration in the Cross that we are utterly powerless to do so. It is a misunderstanding on the one hand of God's demands and on the other hand of the source of supply.

We see the Law and we think that we must meet its claims, but we need to remember that, though the Law in itself is all right, it will be all wrong if it is applied to the wrong person. The "wretched man" of Romans 7 tried to meet the demands of God's law *himself*, and that was the cause of his trouble. The repeated use of the little word "I" in this chapter gives the clue to the failure. "The good which I would I do not: but the evil which I would not, that I practice" (Rom. 7:19). There was a fundamental misconception in this man's mind. He thought God was asking *him* to keep the Law, so of course he was trying to do so, whereas God was requiring no such thing of him. What was the result? Far from doing what pleased God, he found himself doing what displeased him. In his very efforts to do the will of God he did exactly the opposite of what he knew to be his will.

I Thank God!

Romans 6 deals with "the body of sin," Romans 7 with "the body of this death" (6:6; 7:24). In chapter 6 the whole question before us is sin; in chapter 7 the whole question before us is death. What is the difference between the body of sin and the body of death? In regard to sin (that is, to whatever displeases God) I have a body of sin—a body, that is to say, which is actively engaged in sin. But in regard to the Law of God (that is, to that which expresses the will of God) I have a body of death. My activity in regard to sin makes my body a body of sin; my failure in regard to God's will makes my body a body of death. In regard to all that is wicked, worldly, and Satanic, I am, in my nature, wholly positive; but in regard to all that pertains to holiness and Heaven and God, I am wholly negative.

Have you discovered the truth of that in your life? It is no good merely to discover it in Romans 6 and 7. Have you discovered that you carry the

encumbrance of a lifeless body in regard to God's will? You have no difficulty in speaking about worldly matters, but when you try to speak for the
Lord you are tongue-tied; when you try to pray you feel sleepy; when you
try to do something for the Lord you feel unwell. You can do anything but
that which relates to God's will. There is something in this body that does
not harmonize with the will of God.

What does death mean? We may illustrate from a well-known verse
in the first letter to the Corinthians: "For this cause many among you are
weak and sickly, and not a few sleep" (1 Corinthians 11:30). Death is
weakness produced to its extremity—weakness, sickness, death. Death
means utter weakness; it means you are weak to such a point that you can
become no weaker. That I have a body of death in relation to God's will
means that I am so weak when it comes to serving God, so utterly weak,
that I am reduced to a point of dire helplessness. "O wretched man that I
am! who shall deliver me out of the body of this death?" cried Paul, and it
is good when anyone cries out as he did. There is nothing more musical in
the ears of the Lord. This cry is the most spiritual and the most scriptural
cry a man can utter. He only utters it when he knows he can do nothing,
and gives up making any further resolutions. Up to this point, every time
he failed he made a new resolution and doubled and redoubled his will-
power. At last he discovers there is no use in his making up his mind any
more, and he cries out in desperation: "O wretched man that I am !" Like
someone who awakes suddenly to find himself in a burning building, his
cry is now for help, for he has come to the point where he despairs of
himself.

Have you despaired of yourself, or do you hope that if you read and pray
more you will be a better Christian? Bible-reading and prayer are not wrong,
and God forbid that we should suggest that they are, but *it is wrong to trust
even in them for victory.* Our help is in him who is the object of that reading
and prayer. Our trust must be in Christ alone. Happily the "wretched man"
does not merely deplore his wretchedness; he asks a fine question, namely:
"Who shall deliver me?" "*Who?*" Hitherto he has looked for some thing; now
his hope is in a Person. Hitherto he has looked within for a solution to his
problem; now he looks beyond himself for a Savior. He no longer puts forth
self-effort; all his expectation is now in Another.

How did we obtain forgiveness of sins? Was it by reading, praying, almsgiving, and so on? No, we looked to the Cross, believing in what the Lord Jesus had done; and deliverance from sin becomes ours on exactly the same principle, nor is it otherwise with the question of pleasing God. In the matter of forgiveness we look to Christ on the Cross; in the matter of deliverance from sin and of doing the will of God we look to Christ in our hearts. For the one we depend on what he has done; for the other we depend on what he will do in us; but in regard to both, our dependence is on him alone. From start to finish, he is the One who does it all.

At the time when the Epistle to the Romans was written a murderer was punished in a peculiar and terrible manner. The dead body of the one murdered was tied to the living body of the murderer, head to head, hand to hand, foot to foot, and the living one was bound to the dead one till death. The murderer could go where he pleased, but wherever he went he had to carry the corpse of that murdered man with him. Could [any other] punishment be more appalling? Yet this is the illustration Paul now uses. It is as though he were bound to a dead body—his own "body of death"—and unable to get free. Wherever he goes, he is hampered by this terrible burden. At last he can bear it no longer, and cries: "O wretched man that I am! who shall deliver me . . . ?" And then, in a flash of illumination, his cry of despair changes to a song of praise. He has found the answer to his question. "I thank God through Jesus Christ our Lord" (Rom. 7:25).

We know that justification is ours through the Lord Jesus and requires no work on our part, but we think sanctification is dependent on our own efforts. We know we can receive forgiveness only by entire reliance on the Lord; yet we believe we can obtain deliverance by doing something ourselves. We fear that if we do nothing, nothing will happen. After salvation the old habit of "doing" reasserts itself and we begin our old self-efforts again. Then God's word comes afresh to us: "It is finished" (John 19:30). He has done everything on the Cross for our forgiveness and he will do everything in us for our deliverance. In both cases he is the doer. "It is *God* that worketh in you."

The first words of the delivered man are very precious—"I thank God." If someone gives you a cup of water you thank the person who gave it, not someone else. Why did Paul say "Thank God"? Because God was the One who did everything. Had it been Paul who did it, he would have said, "Thank Paul." But he saw that Paul was a "wretched man" and that God alone could meet his need; so he said, "Thank God." God wants to do all the work, for he must have all the glory. If we do some of the work, then we could claim some of the glory ourselves. But God must have it all. He does all the work from beginning to end.

What we have said in this chapter might seem negative and unpractical if we were to stop at this point, as though the Christian life were a matter of sitting still and waiting for something to happen. Of course it is very far from being so. All who truly live it know it to be a matter of very positive and active faith in Christ and in an altogether new principle of life—the law of the Spirit of life. We are now going to look at the effects in us of this new life principle.

CHAPTER 10

The Path of Progress: Walking in the Spirit

Coming now to Romans 8, we may first summarize the argument of our second section of the letter from chapter 5:12 to chapter 8:39 in two phrases, each containing a contrast and each marking an aspect of Christian experience. They are:

Romans 5:12 to 6:23: "In Adam" and "in Christ."

Romans 7:1 to 8:39: "In the flesh" and "in the Spirit."

We need to understand the relationship of these four things. The former two are "objective" and set forth our *position*, firstly as we were by nature, and secondly as we now are by faith in the redemptive work of Christ. The latter two are "subjective" and relate to our *walk* as a matter of practical experience. Scripture makes it clear that the first two give us only a part of the picture and that the second two are required to complete it. We think it enough to be "in Christ," but we learn now that we must also walk "in the Spirit" (Rom. 8:9). The frequent occurrence of "the Spirit" in the early part of Romans 8 serves to emphasize this further important lesson of the Christian life.

The Flesh and the Spirit

The flesh is linked with Adam; the Spirit with Christ. Leaving aside now as settled the question of whether we are in Adam or in Christ, the time has come to ask ourselves: "Am I living in the flesh or in the Spirit?"

To live in the flesh is to do something "out from"[1] myself as in Adam. It is to derive strength from the old natural source of life that I inherited from him, so that I enjoy in experience all Adam's very complete provision for sinning, which all of us have found so effective. Now the same is true of what is in Christ. To enjoy in experience what is true of me as in him, I must learn what it is to walk in the Spirit. It is a historic fact that in Christ my old man was crucified, and it is a present fact that I am blessed "with every spiritual blessing in the heavenly places in Christ" (Eph. 1:3); but if I do not live in the Spirit, then my life may be quite a contradiction of the fact that I am in Christ, for what is true of me in him is not expressed in me. I may recognize that I am in Christ, but I may also have to face the fact that, for example, my old temper is very much in evidence.

What is the trouble? It is that I am holding the truth merely objectively, whereas what is true objectively must be made true subjectively; and that is brought about as I live in the Spirit.

Not only am I in Christ, but Christ is in me. And just as, physically, a man cannot live and work in water but only in air, so spiritually Christ dwells and manifests himself not in terms of "flesh" but of "spirit." Therefore if I live "after the flesh," I find that what is mine in Christ is, so to say, held in suspense in me. Though *in fact* I am in Christ, yet if I live in the flesh—that is, in my own strength and under my own direction—then *in experience* I find, to my dismay, that it is what is in Adam that manifests itself in me. If I would know in experience all that is in Christ, then I must learn to live in the Spirit.

Living in the Spirit means that I trust the Holy Spirit to do in me what I cannot do myself. This life is completely different from the life I would naturally live of myself. Each time I am faced with a new demand from the Lord, I look to him to do in me what he requires of me. It is not a case of *trying* but of *trusting;* not of *struggling* but of *resting in him.* If I have a hasty

---

[1] The author has in mind the Greek preposition *ek*, the sense of which is not easily conveyed by any single English word.—*Angus Kinnear*

temper, impure thoughts, a quick tongue, or a critical spirit, I shall not set out with a determined effort to change myself, but, instead, reckoning myself dead in Christ to these things, I shall look to the Spirit of God to produce in me the needed purity of humility or meekness, confident that he will do so. This is what it means to "stand still, and see the salvation of the Lord, which he will work for you" (Exod. 14:13).

Some of you have no doubt had an experience something like the following. You have been asked to go and see a friend, and you knew the friend was not very friendly, but you trusted the Lord to see you through. You told him before you set out that in yourself you could not but fail, and you asked him for all that was needed. Then, to your surprise, you did not feel at all irritated, though your friend was far from gracious. On your return you thought over the experience and marveled that you had kept so calm, and you wondered if you would be just as calm next time. You were amazed at yourself and sought an explanation. This is the explanation: *the Holy Spirit carried you through.*

Unfortunately, we only have this kind of experience once in a while, but it should be ours constantly. When the Holy Spirit takes things in hand, there is no need for strain on our part. It is not a case of clenching our teeth and thinking that thus we have controlled ourselves beautifully and have had a glorious victory. No, where there is a real victory, it is not fleshly effort that carries us through, but the Lord.

The object of temptation is always to get us to do something. During the first three months of the Japanese war in China, we lost a great many tanks and so were unable to deal with the Japanese tanks, until the following scheme was devised. A single shot would be fired at a Japanese tank by one of our snipers in ambush. After a considerable lapse of time the first shot would be followed by a second; then, after a further silence, by another shot; until the tank driver, eager to locate the source of the disturbance, would pop his head out to look around. The next shot, carefully aimed, would put an end to him.

As long as he remained under cover he was perfectly safe. The whole scheme was devised to bring him out into the open. In the same way, Satan's temptations are not primarily to make us do something particularly sinful, but merely to cause us to act in our own energy; and as soon as we step out of our hiding-place to do something on that basis, he has gained the victory over us. If we do not move, if we do not come out of the cover of Christ into the realm of the flesh, then he cannot get us.

The divine way of victory does not permit of our doing anything at all—anything, that is to say, outside of Christ. This is because as soon as we move, we run into danger, for our natural inclinations take us in the wrong direction. Where, then, are we to look for help? Turn now to Galatians 5:17, "The flesh lusteth against the Spirit, and the Spirit against the flesh." This tells us where the real tussle takes place. The fight with the flesh is not ours but the Holy Spirit's, "for these are contrary the one to the other," and it is he, not we, who meets and deals with it. What is the result? "That ye may not do the things that ye would."

I think we have often failed to grasp the full import of that last clause. Let us consider it for a moment. What "would we do" naturally? We would move off on some course of action dictated by our own instincts and apart from the will of God. The effect, therefore, of our refusal to act out from ourselves is that the Holy Spirit is free to do his work—free, that is, to meet and deal with the flesh in us, so that in fact we do not do what we naturally would do. Instead of going off on a plan and course of our own; we find instead our satisfaction in *His* perfect plan. Hence the command is a positive one: "Walk by the Spirit, and ye shall not fulfill the lust of the flesh" (Gal. 5:16). If we live in the Spirit, if we walk by faith in the risen Christ, we can truly "stand aside" while the Spirit gains new victories over the flesh every day. He has been given to us to take charge of this business. Our victory lies in hiding in Christ, and in counting in simple trust upon his Holy Spirit within us to overcome in us our fleshly lusts with his own new desires. The Cross has been given to procure salvation for us; the Spirit has been given to produce salvation in us. Christ risen and ascended is the basis of our salvation; Christ in our hearts by the Spirit is its power.

Christ Our Life

"I thank God through Jesus Christ!" That exclamation of Paul's is fundamentally the same as his other words in Galatians 2:20, which we have taken as the key to our study: "I live; and yet no longer I, *but Christ*." We saw how prominent is the word "I" throughout Romans 7, culminating in the agonized cry: "O wretched man that *I* am!" Then follows the shout of deliverance: "Thank God . . . *Jesus Christ!*" and it is clear that the discovery Paul has made is this: that *the life we live is the life of Christ alone.* We think of the Christian life as a "changed life," but it is not that. What God offers us is an "exchanged life"—a "substituted life," and Christ is our Substitute within. "I live; and yet no longer I, but Christ liveth in me." This life is not something which we ourselves have to produce. It is Christ's own life reproduced in us.

How many Christians believe in "reproduction" in this sense, as something more than regeneration? Regeneration means that the life of Christ is planted in us by the Holy Spirit at our new birth. "Reproduction" goes further: it means that new life grows and becomes manifest progressively in us, until the very likeness of Christ begins to be reproduced in our lives. That is what Paul means when he speaks of his travail for the Galatians "until Christ be formed in you" (Gal. 4:19).

Let me illustrate with another story. I once stayed in America in the home of a saved couple who soon after my arrival requested me to pray for them. I inquired the case of their trouble.

"Oh, Mr. Nee, we have been in a bad way lately" they confessed. "We are so easily irritated by the children, and during the past few weeks we have both lost our tempers several times a day. We are really dishonoring the Lord. Will you ask him to give us patience?"

"That is the one thing I cannot do," I said.

"What do you mean?" they asked.

"I mean that one thing is certain," I answered, "and that is that God is not going to answer your prayer."

At that they said in amazement, "Do you mean to tell us we have gone so far that God is not willing to hear us when we ask him to make us patient?"

"No, I do not mean quite that, but I would like to ask you if *you* have ever prayed in this respect. You have. But did God answer? No! Do you know why? Because you have no need of patience."

Then the wife's eyes flashed. She said, "What do you mean? We do not need patience, and yet we get irritated the whole day long! It doesn't make sense. What *do* you mean?"

Quietly, I replied, "It is not patience you have need of—it is Christ."

And this is the truth. God will not give me humility or patience or holiness or love as separate gifts of his grace. He is not a retailer dispensing grace to us in packets, measuring out some patience to the impatient, some love to the unloving, some meekness to the proud, in quantities that we take and work on as a kind of capital. He has given only one gift to meet all our needs—His Son Christ Jesus—and as I look to him to live out his life in me, he will be humble and patient and loving and everything else I need—in my stead. Remember the word in the first Epistle of John:

> God gave unto us eternal life, and this life is in his Son. He that hath the Son hath the life; and he that hath not the Son of God hath not the life (1 John 5:11–12).

The life of God is not given us as a separate item; the life of God is given us in the Son. It is "eternal life in Christ Jesus our Lord" (Rom. 6:23). Our relationship to the Son is our relationship to the life.

It is a blessed thing to discover the difference between Christian graces and Christ: to know the difference between meekness and Christ, between patience and Christ, between love and Christ. Remember again what is said in 1 Corinthians 1:30: "Christ Jesus . . . was made unto us wisdom from God, and righteousness and sanctification, and redemption." The common conception of sanctification is that every item of the life should be holy; but that is not holiness, it is the fruit of holiness. Holiness is Christ. It is the Lord Jesus being made over to us to *be* that. So you can put in anything there: love, humility, power, self-control. Today there is a call for patience: he is our patience! Tomorrow the call may be for purity: he is our purity! He is the answer to every need. That is why Paul speaks of "the fruit of the Spirit" as one (Gal. 5:22) and not of "fruits" as separate items. God has given us his Holy Spirit, and when love is needed the fruit of the Spirit is love; when joy is needed the fruit of the Spirit is joy. It is always true. It does not matter what your personal deficiency [is], or whether it is a hundred and one different things: God has one sufficient answer—his Son Jesus Christ—and he is the answer to every human need.

How can we know more of Christ in this way? Only by way of an increasing awareness of need. Some are afraid to discover deficiency in themselves and so they never grow. Growth *in grace* is the only sense in which we can grow; and grace, we have said, is God doing something for us. We all have the same Christ dwelling within, but revelation of some new need will lead us spontaneously to trust him to live out his life in us in that particular [area]. Greater capacity means greater enjoyment of God's supply. Another letting go, a fresh trusting in Christ, and another stretch of land is conquered. "Christ my life" is the secret of enlargement.

We have spoken of trying and trusting, and the difference between the two. Believe me, it is the difference between Heaven and Hell. It is not something just to be talked over as a satisfying thought; it is stark reality. "Lord, I cannot do it, therefore I will no longer try to do it." This is the point most of us fall short of. "Lord, I cannot; therefore I will take my hands off; from now on I trust *thee* for that." We refuse to act; we depend on him to do so, and then we enter fully and joyfully into the action he initiates. It is not passivity; it is a most active life, trusting the Lord like that; drawing life from him, taking him to be our very life, letting him live his life in us as we go forth in his name.

The Law of the Spirit of Life

> There is therefore now no condemnation to them that are in Christ Jesus, who walk not after the flesh, but after the Spirit. For the law of the Spirit of life in Christ Jesus hath made free from the law of sin and death (Rom. 8:1–2, AV).

It is in chapter 8 that Paul presents to us in detail the positive side of life in the Spirit. "There is therefore now no condemnation," he begins, and this statement may at first seem out of place here. Surely condemnation was met by the Blood through which we found peace with God and salvation from wrath (Rom. 5:1, 9). But there are two kinds of condemnation: namely, that before God and that before myself (just as earlier we saw there are two kinds of peace) and the second may at times seem to us even more awful than the first. When I see that the Blood of Christ has satisfied God, then I know my sins are forgiven, and there is for me no more condemnation before God. Yet I may still be knowing defeat, and the sense of inward condemnation on this account may be very real, as Romans 7 shows. But if I have learned to live by Christ as my life, then I have learned the secret of victory, and, praise God! In this inward sense also, "there is therefore now no condemnation." "The mind of the spirit is life and peace" (Rom. 8:6), and this becomes my experience as I learn to walk in the Spirit. With peace in my heart I have no time to feel condemned, but only to praise him who leads me on from one fresh victory to another.

But what lay behind my sense of condemnation? Was it not the experience of defeat and the sense of helplessness to do anything about it? Before I saw that Christ is my life, I labored under a constant sense of handicap; limitation dogged my steps; I felt disabled at every turn. I was always crying out: "I cannot do this! I cannot do that!" Try as I would, I had to acknowledge that I "cannot please God" (Rom. 8:8). But there is no "I cannot" in Christ. Now it is: "I can do all things in him that strengtheneth me" (Phil. 4:13).

How can Paul be so daring? On what grounds does he declare that he is now free from limitation and "can do all things"? Here is his answer: "For the law of the Spirit of life in Christ Jesus made me free from the law of sin and of death" (Rom. 8:2). Why is there no more condemnation? "*For* . . ." says Paul. There is a reason for it; there is something definite to account for it. And the reason is that a law called "the law of the Spirit of life" has proved stronger than another law called "the law of sin and death." What are these laws? How do they operate? And what is the difference between sin and the law of sin, and between death and the law of death?

First let us ask ourselves, "What is a law?" Well, strictly speaking, a law is a generalization examined until it is proved that there is no exception. We might define it more simply as something which happens over and over again. Each time the thing happens, it happens in the same way. We can illustrate this both from statutory and from natural law. For example, in Britain, if I drive a car on the right hand side of the road, the traffic police will stop me. Why? Because it is against the law of the land. If *you* do it, you will be stopped too. Why? For the same reason that I would be stopped: it is against the law and the law makes no exceptions. It is something which happens repeatedly and unfailingly. Or again, we all know what is meant by gravity. If I drop my handkerchief in London it falls to the ground. That is the effect of gravity. But the same is true if I drop it in New York or Hong Kong. No matter where I let it go, gravity operates, and it always produces the same results. Whenever the same conditions prevail, the same effects are seen. There is thus a "law" of gravity.

Now what of the law of sin and death? If someone passes an unkind remark about me, at once something goes wrong inside me. That is not law; that is sin. But if, when different people pass unkind remarks, the same "something" goes wrong inside, then I discern a law within—a law of sin. Like the law of gravity, it is something constant. It always works the same way. And so too with the law of death. Death, we have said, is weakness produced to its limit. Weakness is "I cannot." Now, if when I try to please God in this particular matter I find I cannot, and if, when I try to please him in that other thing I again find I cannot, then I discern a law at work. There is not only sin in me, but a *law* of sin; there is not only death in me, but a *law* of death.

Then again, not only is gravity a law in the sense that it is constant, admitting of no exception, but, unlike the rule of the road, it is a "natural" law and not the subject of discussion and decision, but of discovery. The law is there, and the handkerchief "naturally" drops of itself without any help from me. And the "law" discovered by the man in Romans 7:23 is just like that. It is a law of sin and of death, opposed to that which is good, and crippling the man's will to do good. He "naturally" sins according to the "law of sin" in his members. He wills to be different, but that law in him is relentless and no human will can resist it. So this brings me to the question, "How can I be set free from the law of sin and death?" I need deliverance from sin, and still more do I need deliverance from death, but most of all I need deliverance from the *law* of sin and of death. How can I be delivered from the constant repetition of weakness and failure? In order to answer this question, let us follow out our two illustrations further.

One of our great burdens in China used to be the *likin* tax, a law which none could escape, originating in the Ch'in Dynasty and operating right down to our own day. It was an inland tax on the transit of goods, applied throughout the empire and having numerous barriers for collection, and officers enjoying very large powers. The result was that the charge on goods passing through several provinces might become very heavy indeed. But a few years ago a second law came into operation which set aside the *likin* law. Can you imagine the feelings of relief in those who had suffered under the old law? Now there was no need to think or hope or pray; the new law was already there and had delivered us from the old law. No longer was there need to think beforehand what one would say if one met a *likin* officer tomorrow!

And as with the law of the land, so it is with natural law. How can the law of gravity be annulled? With regard to my handkerchief, that law is at work clearly enough, pulling it down, but I have only to place my hand under the handkerchief and it does not drop. Why? The law is still there. I do not deal with the law of gravity; in fact I *cannot* deal with the law of gravity. Then why does my handkerchief not fall to the ground? Because there is a power keeping it from doing so. The law is there, but another law superior to it is in operation to overcome it, namely the law of life. Gravity can do its utmost, but the handkerchief will not drop, because another law is working against the law of gravity to maintain it there. We have all seen the tree which was once a small seed fallen between the slabs of a paving, and which has grown until heavy stone blocks have been lifted by the power of the life within it. That is what we mean by the triumph of one law over another.

In just such a manner God delivers us from one law by introducing another law. The law of sin and death is there all the time, but God has put another law into operation—the law of the Spirit of life in Christ Jesus: and that law is strong enough to deliver us from the law of sin and death. It is, you see, a law of *life in Christ*—the resurrection life that in him has met death in all its forms and triumphed over it (Eph. 1:19–20). The Lord Jesus dwells in our hearts in the person of his Holy Spirit, and if, committing ourselves to him, we let him have a clear way, we shall find his new law of lie superseding that old law. We shall learn what it is to be kept, not by our own insufficient strength, but "by the power of God" (1 Peter 1:5).

The Manifestation of the Law of Life

Let us seek to make this practical. We touched earlier on the matter of our will in relation to the things of God. Even older Christians do not realize how great a part will-power plays in their lives. That was part of Paul's trouble in Romans 7. His will was good, but all his actions contradicted it, and however much he made up his mind and set himself to please God, it led him only into worse darkness. "I *would* do good," but "I *am* carnal, sold under sin." That is the point. Like a car without petrol, that has to be pushed, and that stops as soon as it is left alone, many

Christians endeavor to drive themselves by will-power, and then think the Christian life a most exhausting and bitter one. Some even force themselves to do Christian things because others do them, while admitting there is no meaning in it to them. They force themselves to be what they are not, and it is worse than trying to make water run up-hill. For after all, the very highest point the will can reach is that of willingness (Matt. 26:41).

If we have to exert so much effort in our Christian living, it simply says that we are not really like that at all. We don't need to force ourselves to speak our native language. In fact we only have to exert will-power in order to do things we *do not* do naturally. We may do them for a time, but the law of sin and death wins in the end. We may be able to say: "To will is present with me, and I perform that which is good for two weeks," but eventually we shall have to confess: "How to perform it I know not." No, what I already am, I do not long to be. If I "would" it is because I am not.

You ask, "Why do men use will-power to try to please God?" There may be two reasons. They may, of course, never have experienced the new birth, in which case they have no new life to draw upon; or they may have been born again and the life be there, but they have not learned to trust in that life. It is this lack of understanding that results in habitual failure and sinning, bringing them to the place where they almost cease to believe in the possibility of anything better.

But because we have not believed fully, that does not mean that the feeble life we intermittently experience is all God has given us. Romans 6:23 states that "the free gift of God is eternal life in Christ Jesus our Lord," and now in Romans 8:2 we read that "the law of the Spirit of life in Christ Jesus" has come to our aid. So Romans 8:2 speaks not of a new gift, but of the life already referred to in Romans 6:23. In other words, it is *a new revelation of what we already have*. I feel I cannot emphasize this too much. It is not something fresh from God's hand, but a new unveiling of what he has already given. It is a new discovery of a work already done in Christ, for the words "made me free" are in the past tense. If I really see this and put my faith in him, there is no absolute necessity for the experience of Romans 7—either the unhappy struggle and failure or the fruitless display of will-power—to be repeated in me.

If we will let go our own wills and trust him, we shall not fall to the ground and break, but we shall fall into *a different law,* the law of the Spirit of life. For God has given us not only life but a law of life. And just as the law of gravity is a natural law and not the result of human legislation, so the law of life is a "natural" law, similar in principle to the law that keeps our heart beating or that controls the movement of our eyelids. There is no need for us to think about our eyes, or to decide that we must blink every so often to keep them cleansed; and still less do we bring our will to bear upon our heart-beat. Indeed, to do so might rather harm than help it. No, so long as it has life, it works spontaneously. Our wills only interfere with the law of life. I discovered that fact once in the following way.

I used to suffer from sleeplessness. Once after several sleepless nights, when I had prayed much about it and exhausted all my resources, I confessed at length to God that the fault must lie with me and asked to be shown where. I said to God: "I demand an explanation." He answer was: "Believe in nature's laws." Sleep is as much a law as hunger is, and I realized that, though I had never thought of worrying whether I would get hungry or not, I had been worrying about sleeping. I had been trying to help nature, and that is the chief trouble with most sufferers from sleeplessness. But now I trusted not only God but God's law of nature, and very soon slept well.

Should we not read the Bible? Of course we should, or our spiritual life will suffer. But that should not mean forcing ourselves to read. There is a new law in us which gives us a hunger for God's Word. *Then* half an hour can be more profitable than five hours of forced reading. And it is the same with giving, with preaching, with testimony. Forced preaching is apt to result in preaching a warm gospel with a cold heart, and we all know what men mean by "cold charity."

If we will let ourselves live in the new law, we shall be less conscious of the old. It is still there, but it is no longer governing and we are no longer in its grip. That is why the Lord says in Matthew 6: "Behold the birds . . . Consider the lilies." If we could ask the birds whether they were not afraid of the law of gravity, how would they reply? They would say: "We never heard the name of Newton. We know nothing about his law. We fly because it is the law of our life to fly." Not only is there in them a life with the power of flight, but that life has a law which enables these living creatures quite spontaneously and consistently to overcome the law of gravity. Yet gravity remains. If you get up early one morning when the cold is intense and the snow thick on the ground, and there is a dead sparrow in the courtyard, you are reminded at once of the persistence of that law. But while birds live, they overcome it, and the life within them is what dominates their consciousness.

God has been truly gracious to us. He has given us this new law of the Spirit, and for us to "fly" is no longer a question of our will, but of his life. Have you noticed what a trial it is to make an impatient Christian patient? To require patience of him is enough to make him ill with depression. But God has never told us to force ourselves to be what we are not naturally: to try by taking thought to add to our spiritual stature. Worrying may possibly decrease a man's height, but it certainly never added anything to it. "Be not anxious," are his words. "Consider the lilies, . . . they *grow*." He is directing our attention to the new law of life in us. Oh, for a new appreciation of the life that is ours!

What a precious discovery this is! It can make altogether new men of us, for it operates in the smallest things as well as in the bigger ones. It checks us when, for example, we put out a hand to look at a book in someone else's room, reminding us that we have not asked permission and have no right to do so. We cannot, the Holy Spirit tells us, encroach thus upon the rights of others.

Once I was talking to a Christian friend and he turned to me and said: "Do you know, I believe that if anyone is willing to live by the law of the Spirit of Life, such a man will become truly refined."

"What do you mean?" I asked.

He replied:

That law has the power to make a man a perfect gentleman. Some scornfully say: "you can't blame those people for the way they act; they are just country folk and have no educational advantages." But the real question is, "Have they the life of the Lord within?" For I tell you, *that* life can say to them: "Your voice is too loud," or, "That laughter was not right," or, "Your motive in passing that remark was wrong." In a thousand details the Spirit of Life can tell them how to act, so producing in them a true re-finement. There is no such inherent power in education.

And yet my friend was himself an educationalist!

But it is true. Take, for example, talkativeness. Are you a person of too many words? When you stay with people, do you say to yourself:

> What shall I do? I am a Christian; but if I am to glorify the name of the Lord, I simply *must not* talk so much. So today let me be extra careful to hold myself in check?

And for an hour or two you succeed—until on some pretext you loose control and, before you know where you are, find yourself once again in difficulty with your garrulous tongue. Yes, let us be fully assured that the will is useless here. For me to exhort you to exercise your will in this mat-ter would be but to offer you the vain religion of the world, not the life in Christ Jesus. For consider again: a talkative person remains just that, though he keep silent all day, for there is a "natural" law of talkativeness governing him (or her!), just as a peach tree is a peach tree whether or not it bears peaches. But as Christians we discover a new law in us, the law of the spirit of life, which transcends all else, and which has already delivered us from the "law" of our talkativeness. If, believing the Lord's Word, we yield ourselves to that new law, *it* will tell us when we should stop talking—or not start!—and *it* will empower us to do so. On that ba-sis you can go to your friend's house for two or three hours, or stay for two or three days, and experience no difficulty. On your return you will just thank God for his new law of life.

It is this spontaneous life that is the Christian life. It manifests itself in love for the unlovely—for the brother whom on natural grounds we would not like and certainly could not love. It works on the basis of what the Lord sees of possibility in that brother. "Lord, *you* see he is lovable and *you* love him. Love him, now, through me!" And it manifests itself in reality of life—in a true genuineness of moral character. There is too much hypoc-risy in the lives of Christians, too much play-acting. Nothing takes away from the effectiveness of Christian witness as does a pretense of something that is not really there, for the man in the street unfailingly penetrates such a disguise in the end and finds us out for what we are. Yes, pretense gives way to reality when we trust the law of life.

The Fourth Step: "Walk . . . After the Spirit"

For what the law could not do, in that it was weak through the flesh, God, sending his own Son in the likeness of sinful flesh and as an offering for sin, condemned sin in the flesh: that the ordinance of the law might be fulfilled in us, who walk not after the flesh, but after the Spirit (Rom. 8:3–4).

Every careful reader of these two verses will see that there are two things presented here. They are, firstly, what the Lord Jesus has done *for* us, and secondly, what the Holy Spirit will do *in* us. "The flesh" is "weak"; consequently the ordinance of the law cannot be fulfilled in us "after the flesh." (Remember, it is again here a question not of salvation but of pleasing God.) Now, because of our inability, God took two steps. In the first place, he intervened to deal with the heart of our problem. He sent his Son in the flesh, who died for sin and in doing so "condemned sin in the flesh." That is to say, he took to death representatively all that belonged to the old creation in us, whether we speak of it as "our old man," "the flesh," or the carnal "I." Thus God struck at the very root of our trouble by removing the fundamental grounds of our weakness. This was the first step.

But still "the ordinance of the law" remained to be fulfilled "in us." How could this be done? It required God's further provision of the indwelling Holy Spirit. It is he who is sent to take care of the inward side of this thing, and he is able to do so, we are told, as we "walk . . . after the Spirit."

What does it mean to walk after the Spirit? It means two things. Firstly, it is not a *work*; it is a *walk*. Praise God, the burdensome and fruitless effort I involved myself in when I sought "in the flesh" to please God gives place to a quiet and restful dependence on "his working, which worketh in me mightily" (Col. 1:29). That is why Paul contrasts the "works" of the flesh with the "fruit" of the Spirit (Gal. 5:19–22).

Then secondly, to "walk after" implies subjection. Walking after the flesh means that I yield to the dictates of the flesh, and the following verses in Romans 8:5–8 make clear where that leads me. It only brings me into conflict with God. To walk after the Spirit is to be subject to the Spirit. There is one thing that the man who walks after the Spirit cannot do, and that is be independent of Him. I *must* be subject to the Holy Spirit. The initiative of my life must be with him. Only as I yield myself to obey him shall I find the "law of the Spirit of life" in full operation, and the "ordinance of the law" (all that I have been trying to do to please God) being fulfilled—no longer *by* me but *in* me. "As many as are led by the Spirit of God, these are sons of God" (Rom. 8:14).

We are all familiar with the words of the benediction in 2 Corinthians 13:14: "The grace of the Lord Jesus Christ, and the love of God, and the communion of the Holy Ghost, be with you all." The love of God is the source of all spiritual blessing; the grace of the Lord Jesus has made it possible for that spiritual wealth to become ours; and the communion of the Holy Ghost is the means whereby it is imparted to us. Love is something hidden in the heart of God; grace is that love expressed and made available in the Son; communion is the impartation of that grace by the Spirit. What the Father has devised concerning us, the Son has accomplished for us, and now the Holy Spirit communicates it to us. When therefore we discover something fresh that the Lord Jesus has procured for us in his Cross, let us look, for its realization, in the direction that God has indicated, and, by our steadfast obedience to the Holy Spirit, keep wide open the way for him to impart it to us. That is his ministry. He has come for that very purpose—that he may make real in us all that is ours through the finished work of Christ.

We have learned in China that, when leading a soul to Christ, we must be very thorough, for there is no certainty when he will again have the help of other Christians. We always seek to make it clear to a new believer that, when he has asked the Lord to forgive his sins and to come into his life, his heart has become the residence of a living Person. The Holy Spirit of God is now within him, to open to him the Scriptures that he may find Christ there, to direct his prayer, to govern his life, and to reproduce in him the character of his Lord.

I remember, late one summer, I went for a prolonged period of rest to a hill-resort, where accommodation was difficult to obtain, and while there it was necessary for me to sleep in one house and take my meals in another, the latter being the home of a mechanic and his wife. For the first two weeks of my visit, apart from asking a blessing at each meal, I said nothing to my hosts about the Gospel; and then one day my opportunity came to tell them about the Lord Jesus. They were ready to listen and to come to him in simple faith for the forgiveness of their sins. They were born again, and a new light and joy came into their lives, for theirs was a real conversion. I took care to make clear to them what had happened, and then, as the weather turned colder, the time came for me to leave them and return to Shanghai.

During the cold winter months the man was in the habit of drinking wine with his meals, and he was apt to do so to excess. After my departure, with the return of the cold weather, the wine appeared on the table again, and that day, as he had become accustomed to do, the husband bowed his head to return thanks for the meal—but no words would come. After one or two vain attempts he turned to his wife. "What is wrong?" he asked. "Why cannot we pray today? Fetch the Bible and see what it has to say about wine drinking." I had left a copy of the Scriptures with them, but though the wife could read, she was ignorant of the Word, and she turned the pages in vain seeking for light on the subject. They did not know how to consult God's Book, and it was impossible to consult God's messenger, for I was many miles away and it might be months before they could see me. "Just drink your wine," said his wife. "We'll refer the matter to brother Nee at the first opportunity." But still the man found he just could not return thanks to the Lord for that wine. "Take it away!" he said at length; and when she had done so, together they asked a blessing on their meal.

When eventually the man was able to visit Shanghai, he told me the story. Using an expression familiar in Chinese: "Brother Nee," he said, "Resident Boss[2] wouldn't let me have that drink!"

"Very good, brother," I said. "You always listen to Resident Boss!"

Many of us know that Christ is our life. We believe that the Spirit of God is resident in us, but this fact has little effect upon our behavior. The question is, do we know him as a living Person, and do we know him as "Boss"?

---

[2] "Resident Boss"—The author's own rendering of *li-mien tang-chia tih.—Angus Kinnear*

CHAPTER 11

One Body in Christ

Before we pass on to our last important subject, we will review some of the ground we have covered and summarize the steps taken. We have sought to make things simple, and to explain clearly some of the experiences which Christians commonly pass through. But it is clear that the new discoveries that we make as we walk with the Lord are many, and we must be careful to avoid the temptation to over-simplify the work of God. To do so may lead us into serious confusion.

There are children of God who believe that all our salvation, in which they would include the matter of leading a holy life, lies in an appreciation of the value of the precious Blood. They rightly emphasize the importance of keeping short accounts with God over known specific sins, and the continual efficacy of the Blood to deal with sins committed, but they think of the Blood as doing everything. They believe in a holiness which in fact means only separation of the man from his past; that, through the up-to-date blotting out of what he has done on the grounds for the shed Blood, God separates a man out of the world to be his, and

133

that is holiness; and they stop there. Thus they stop short of God's basic demands, and so of the full provision he has made. I think we have by now seen clearly the inadequacy of this.

Then there are those who go further and see that God has included them in the death of his Son on the Cross, in order to deliver them from sin and the Law by dealing with the old man. These are they who really exercise faith in the Lord, for they glory in Christ Jesus and have ceased to put confidence in the flesh (Phil. 3:3). In them God has a clear foundation on which to build. And from this as starting-point, many have gone further still and recognized that consecration (using that word in the truest sense) means giving themselves without reserve into his hands and following him. All these are first steps, and starting from them, we have already touched upon other phases of experience set before us by God and enjoyed by many. It is always essential for us to remember that, while each of them is a precious fragment of truth, no single one of them is by itself the whole of truth. All come to us as the fruit of the work of Christ on the Cross, and we cannot afford to ignore any.

A Gate and a Path

Recognizing a number of such phases in the life and experience of a believer, we note now a further fact, namely that, though these phases do not necessarily occur always in a fixed and precise order, they seem to be marked by certain recurring steps or features. What are these steps? First there is *revelation*. As we have seen, this always precedes *faith* and *experience*. Through his Word, God opens our eyes to the truth of some fact concerning his Son, and then only, as in faith we accept that fact for ourselves, does it become actual as experience in our lives. Thus we have:

1. Revelation (objective).

2. Experience (subjective).

Then further, we note that such experience usually takes the two-fold form of a crisis leading to a continuous process. It is most helpful to think of this in terms of John Bunyan's "wicket gate" through which Christian entered upon a "narrow path." Our Lord Jesus spoke of such a gate and a path leading unto life (Matt. 7:14), and experience accords with this. So now we have:

1. Revelation
2. Experience:
    a. A wicket gate (Crisis)
    b. A narrow path (Process)

Now let us take some of the subjects we have been dealing with and see how this helps us to understand them. We will take first our *justification* and *new birth*. This begins with a *revelation* of the Lord Jesus in his atoning work for our sins on the Cross; there follows the crisis of repentance and faith (the wicket gate), whereby we are initially "made nigh" to God (Eph. 2:13); and this leads us into a walk of maintained fellowship with him *(the narrow path)*, for which the grounds for our day-to-day access is still the precious Blood (Heb 10:19, 22).

When we come to *deliverance from sin*, we again have three steps: the Holy Spirit's work of revelation, or "knowing" (Rom. 6:6); the crisis of faith, or "reckoning" (Rom. 6:11); and the continuing process of consecration, or "presenting ourselves" to God (Rom. 6:13) on the basis of a walk in newness of life.

Consider next *the gift of the Holy Spirit*. This too begins with a new "seeing" of the Lord Jesus as exalted to the throne, which issues in the dual experience of the Spirit outpoured and the Spirit in dwelling.

Going a stage further, to the matter of *pleasing God*, we find again the need for spiritual illumination, that we may see the values of the Cross in regard to "the flesh"—the entire self-life of man. Our acceptance of this by faith leads at once to a "wicket gate" experience (Rom. 7:25), in which we initially cease from "doing" and accept by faith the mighty working of the life of Christ to satisfy God's practical demands in us. This in turn leads us into the "narrow path" of a walk in obedience to the Spirit (Rom. 8:4).

The picture is not identical in each case, and we must beware of forcing any rigid pattern upon the Holy Spirit's working; but perhaps any new experience will come to us more or less on these lines. There will certainly always be first an opening of our eyes to some new aspect of Christ and his finished work, and then faith will open a gate into a pathway. Remember, too, that our division of Christian experience into various subjects: justification, new birth, the gift of the spirit, deliverance, sanctification, etc., is for our clearer understanding only. It does not mean that these stages must or will always follow one another in a certain prescribed order. In fact, if a full presentation of Christ and his Cross is made to us at the very outset, we may well step into a great deal of experience from the first day of our Christian life, even though the full explanation of much of it may only follow later. Would that all Gospel preaching were of such a kind!

One thing is certain, that revelation will always precede faith. Seeing and believing are two principles which govern Christian living. When we see something that God has *done* in Christ, our natural response is: "Thank you, Lord!" and faith follows spontaneously. Revelation is always the work of the Holy Spirit, who is given to come along-side and, by opening the Scriptures to us, to guide us into all the truth (John 16:13). Count upon him, for he is here for that very thing; and when such difficulties as lack of understanding or lack of faith confront you, address those difficulties directly to the Lord—"Lord, open my eyes. Lord, make this new thing clear to me. Lord, help Thou my unbelief!" He will not let such prayers go unheeded.

The Fourfold Work of Christ in His Cross

We are now in a position to go a step further still and to consider how great a range is compassed by the Cross of the Lord Jesus Christ. In the light of Christian experience and for the purpose of analysis, it may help us if we recognize four aspects of God's redemptive work. But in doing so it is essential to keep in mind that the Cross of Christ is *one divine work,* and not many. Once in Judea two thousand years ago the Lord Jesus died and rose again, and he is now "by the right hand of God exalted" (Acts 2:33). The work is finished and need never be repeated, nor can it be added to.

Of the four aspects of the Cross which we shall now mention, we have already dealt with three in some detail. The last will be considered in the two succeeding chapters of our study. They may be briefly summarized as follows:

1. *The Blood of Christ* to deal with sins and guilt.
2. *The Cross of Christ* to deal with sin, the flesh and the natural man.

3. *The Life of Christ* made available to indwell, re-create and empower man.

4. *The Working of Death* in the natural man that that indwelling Life may be progressively manifest.

The first two of these aspects are remedial. They relate to the undoing of the work of the Devil and the undoing of the sin of man. The last two are not remedial but positive, and relate more directly to the securing of the purpose of God. The first two are concerned with recovering what Adam lost by the Fall; the last two are concerned with bringing us into, and bringing into us, something that Adam never had. Thus we see that the achievement of the Lord Jesus in his death and resurrection comprises both a work which provided for the redemption of man and a work which made possible the realization of the purpose of God.

We have dealt at some length in earlier chapters with the two aspects of his death represented by the Blood for sins and guilt and the Cross for sin and the flesh. In our discussion of the eternal purpose, we have also looked briefly at the third aspect—that represented by Christ as the grain of wheat—and we have just seen something of its practical outworking in our last chapter, when considering Christ as our life. Before, however, we pass on to the fourth aspect, which I shall call "bearing the cross," we must say a little more about this third side, namely, the release of the risen life in Christ to indwell man and empower him for service.

We have spoken already of the purpose of God in creation, and have said that it embraced far more than Adam ever came to enjoy. What was that purpose? God wanted to have a race of men whose members were gifted with a spirit whereby communion would be possible with himself, who is Spirit. That race, possessing God's own life, was to co-operate in securing his purposed end by defeating every possible uprising of the enemy and undoing his evil works. That was the great plan. How will it now be effected? The answer is again to be found in the death of the Lord Jesus. It is a mighty death. It is something positive and purposive, going far beyond the recovery of a lost position; for by it, not only are sin and the old man dealt with and their effects annulled, but something more, something infinitely greater and more far-reaching, is introduced.

The Love of Christ

Now we must have before us two passages of the Word, one from Genesis 2 and one from Ephesians 5, which, considered together, are of great importance in at this point.

> And the Lord God caused a deep sleep to fall upon the man, and he slept; and he took one of his ribs, and closed up the flesh instead thereof: and [from] the rib which the Lord God had taken from the man, made he a woman, and brought her unto the man. And the man said, "This is now bone of my bones, and flesh of my flesh: she shall be called Woman [Heb. *ishshah*], because she was taken out of Man [Heb. *ish*]" (Gen. 2:21–23).

> Husbands, love your wives, even as Christ also loved the church, and gave himself up for it; that he might sanctify it, having cleansed it by the washing of water with the Word, that he might present the church to himself a glorious church, not having spot or wrinkle or any such thing; but that it should be holy and without blemish (Eph. 5:25–27).

In Ephesians 5 we have the only chapter in the Bible which explains the passage in Genesis 2. What we have presented to us in Ephesians is indeed very remarkable, if we reflect upon it. I refer to what is contained in those words: "Christ . . . loved the church." There is something most precious here.

We have been taught to think of ourselves as sinners needing redemption. For generations that has been instilled into us, and we praise the Lord for that as our beginning; but it is not what God has in view as his *end*. God speaks here rather of "a glorious church, not having spot or wrinkle or any such thing; but...holy and without blemish." All too often we have thought of the Church as being merely so many "saved sinners." It *is* that; but we have made the terms almost equal to one another, as though it were *only* that, which is not the case. "Saved sinners"—with that thought you have the whole background of sin and the Fall; but in God's sight the Church is *a divine creation in his Son*. The one is largely individual, the other corporate. With the one, the view is negative, belonging to the past; with the other it is positive, looking forward. The "eternal purpose" is something in the mind of God from eternity concerning his Son, and it has as its objective that the Son should have a Body to express his life. Viewed from that standpoint—from the standpoint of the heart of

God—the Church is something which is beyond sin and has never been touched by sin.

So we have an aspect of the death of the Lord Jesus in Ephesians which we do not have so clearly in other places. In Romans, things are viewed from the standpoint of fallen man, and beginning with "Christ died for sinners, enemies, the ungodly" (Rom. 5) we are led progressively to "the love of Christ" (Rom. 8:35). In Ephesians, on the other hand, the standpoint is that of God "before the foundation of the world" (Eph. 1:4), and the heart of the gospel is: "Christ . . . loved the church, and gave himself up for it" (Eph. 5:25). Thus, in Romans it is "we sinned," and the message is of God's love for sinners (Rom. 5:8); whereas in Ephesians it is "Christ loved," and the love here is the love of husband for wife. That kind of love has fundamentally nothing to do with sin as such. What is in view in this passage is not atonement for sin, but the creation of the Church, for which end it is said that he "gave himself."

There is thus an aspect of the death of the Lord Jesus which is altogether positive and a matter particularly of love to his Church, where the question of sin and sinners does not directly appear. To bring this fact home, Paul takes that incident in Genesis 2 as illustration. Now this is one of the marvelous things in the Word, and if our eyes have been opened to see it, it will certainly call forth from us worship.

From Genesis 3 onwards, from the "coats of skins" to Abel's sacrifice, and on from there through the whole Old Testament, there are numerous types which set forth the death of the Lord Jesus as an atonement for sin; yet the apostle does not appeal here to any of those types of his death, but to this one in Genesis 2. Note that; and then recall that it was not until Genesis 3 that sin came in. There is one type of the death of Christ in the Old Testament which has nothing to do with sin, for it is not subsequent to the Fall but prior to it, and that type is here in Genesis 2. Let us look at it for a moment.

Could we say that Adam was put to sleep because Eve had committed a serious sin? Is that what we have here? Certainly not, for Eve was not yet even created. There were as yet no moral issues involved and no problems at all. No, Adam was put to sleep for the express purpose that something might be taken out of him to be formed into someone else. His sleep was not for her sin but for her *existence*. That is what is taught in these verses. This experience of Adam had as its object the creation of Eve, as something determined in the divine counsels. God wanted a woman [*ishshah*]. He put the man [*ish*] to sleep, took a rib from his side and made it into [*ishshah*], a woman, and brought her to the man. That is the picture which God is giving us. It foreshadows an aspect of the death of the Lord Jesus that is not primarily for atonement, but answerable to the sleep of Adam in this chapter.

God forbid that I should suggest that the Lord Jesus did not die for purposes of atonement. Praise God, he did. We must remember that today we are in fact in Ephesians 5 and not in Genesis 2. Ephesians was written *after* the Fall, to men who had suffered from its effects, and in it we have not only the purpose in Creation but also the scars of the Fall—or there would need to be no mention of "spot or wrinkle." Because we are still on the earth and the Fall is a historic fact, redemption is needed (Eph. 1:7).

But we must always view redemption as an interruption, an "emergency" measure, made necessary by a catastrophic break in the straight line of the purpose of God. Redemption is big enough, wonderful enough, to occupy a very large place in our vision, but God is saying that we should not make redemption to be everything, *as though man were created to be redeemed*. The Fall is indeed a tragic dip downwards in that line of purpose, and the atonement a blessed recovery whereby our sins are blotted out and we are restored; but when it is accomplished, there yet remains a work to be done to bring us into possession of that which Adam never possessed, and to give God what his heart most desires. For God has never forsaken the purpose which is represented by that straight line. Adam was never in possession of the life of God as presented in the tree of life. But because of the one work of the Lord Jesus in his death and resurrection (and we must emphasize again that it is all one work), his life was released to become ours by faith, and we have received more than Adam ever possessed. The very purpose of God is brought within reach of fulfillment in us by our receiving Christ as our life.

Adam was put to sleep. We remember that it is said of believers that they fall asleep, rather than that they die. Why? Because whenever death is mentioned, sin is there in the background. In Genesis 3 sin entered into the world and death through sin, but Adam's sleep preceded that. So the type of the Lord Jesus here is not like other types in the Old Testament. In relation to sin and atonement there is a lamb or a bullock slain; but here Adam was not slain, but only put to sleep *to awake again*. Thus he prefigures a death that is not on account of sin, but that has in view, increase in resurrection. Then too we must note that Eve was not created as a separate entity by a separate creation, parallel to that of Adam. Adam slept, and Eve was created out of Adam. That is God's method with the Church. God's "second Man" has awakened from his "sleep", and his Church is created in him and of him, to draw her life from him and to display that resurrection life.

God has a Son, his only begotten, and he seeks that that Son should have brethren. From the position of *only* begotten, He will become the *first* begotten, and instead of the Son alone, God will have many sons. One grain of wheat has died, and many grains will spring up. The first grain was once the only grain; now it has become the first of many. The Lord Jesus laid down his life, and that life emerged in many lives. These are the Biblical figures we have used hitherto in our study to express this truth. Now, in the figure of Eve, the singular takes the place of the plural. The outcome of the Cross is shown to be a single person: a Bride for the Son. Christ loved the Church and gave himself up for it.

One Living Sacrifice

We have said that there is an aspect of the death of Christ presented to us in Ephesians 5, which differs in some degree from that which we have been studying in Romans. Yet in fact this aspect is the very end to which our study of Romans has been moving, and it is into this that the letter is leading us as we shall now see, for redemption leads us back into God's original line of purpose.

In chapter 8, Paul speaks to us of Christ as the firstborn Son among many Spirit-led "sons of God" (Rom. 8:14).

> For whom he foreknew, he also foreordained to be conformed to the image of his Son, that he might be the firstborn among many brethren: and whom he foreordained, them he also called: and whom he called, them he also justified: and whom he justified, them he also glorified (Rom. 8:29–30).

Here justification is seen to lead on to glory, a glory that is expressed not in one or more individuals but in a plurality: in many who manifest the image of One. And this object of our redemption is further set forth, as we have seen, in "the love of Christ" for his own, which is the subject of the last verses of the chapter (8:35–39). But what is implicit here in chapter 8 becomes explicit as we move over into chapter 12, the subject of which is the Body of Christ.

After the first eight chapters of Romans, which we have been studying, there follows a parenthesis in which God's sovereign dealings with Israel are taken up and dealt with, before the theme of the first chapters is resumed. Thus, for our present purpose, the argument of chapter 12 follows that of chapter 8 and not of chapter 11. We might very simply summarize these chapters thus: Our sins are forgiven (ch. 5), we are dead with Christ (ch. 6), we are by nature utterly helpless (ch. 7), therefore we rely upon the indwelling Spirit (ch. 8). After this, and as a consequence of it: "We . . . are one body in Christ" (ch. 12). It is as though this were the logical outcome of all that has gone before, and the thing to which it has all been leading.

Romans 12 and the following chapters contain some very practical instructions for our life and walk. These are introduced with an emphasis once again on consecration. In chapter 6:13 Paul has said:

> Present yourselves unto God, as alive from the dead, and your members as instruments of righteousness unto God.

But now in chapter 12:1 the emphasis is a little different:

> I beseech you therefore, brethren, by the mercies of God, to present your bodies a living sacrifice, holy, acceptable to God, which is your reasonable service.

This new appeal for consecration is made to us as "brethren," linking us in thought to the "many brethren" of chapter 8:29. It is a call to us for a united step of faith, expressed in terms of the presenting of our bodies as one "living sacrifice" unto God.

This is something that goes beyond the merely individual, for it implies contribution to a whole. The "presenting" is personal, but the sacrifice is corporate; it is one sacrifice. Intelligent service to God is one service. We need never feel our contribution is not needed, for if it contributes to *the* service, God is satisfied. And it is through this kind of service that we prove "what is the good and acceptable and perfect will of God" (ch. 12:2), or, in other words, realize our part in God's eternal purpose in Christ Jesus. So Paul's appeal "to every man that is among you" (12:3) is in the light of this new divine fact, that "we, who are many, are one body in Christ, and severally members one of another" (12:5), and it is on this basis that the practical instructions follow.

The vessel through which the Lord Jesus can reveal himself in this generation is not the individual but the Body. True, "God hath dealt to each man a measure of faith" (12:3), but alone in isolation man can never fulfill God's purpose. It requires a complete Body to attain to the stature of Christ and to display his glory. Oh, that we might really see this!

So Romans 12:3–6 draws from the figure of the human body the lesson of our inter-dependence. Individual Christians are not the Body. They are its members, and in a human body "all the members have not the same office." The ear must not imagine itself to be an eye. No amount of prayer will give sight to the ear—but the whole body can see through the eye. So (speaking figuratively) I may have only the gift of hearing, but I can see through others who have the gift of sight; or, perhaps I can walk but cannot work, so I receive help from the hands. An all-too-common attitude to the things of the Lord is that, "What I know, I know; and what I don't know, I don't know, and can do quite well without." But in Christ, the things we do not know, others do, and we may know them and enter into the enjoyment of them through others.

Let me stress that this is not just a comfortable thought. It is a vital factor in the life of God's people. We cannot get along without one another. That is why fellowship in prayer is so important. Prayer together brings in the help of the Body, as must be clear from Matthew 18:19–20. Trusting the Lord by myself may not be enough. I must trust him with others. I must learn to pray "*Our* Father . . . " on the basis of oneness with the Body, for without the help of the Body I cannot get through. In the sphere of service, this is even more apparent. Alone I cannot serve the Lord effectively, and he will spare no pains to teach me this. He will bring things to an end, allowing doors to close and leaving me ineffectively knocking my head against a blank wall until I realize that I need the help of the Body as well as of the Lord. For the life of Christ is the life of the Body, and his gifts are given to us for work that builds up the Body.

The Body is not an illustration but a fact. The Bible does not just say that the Church is *like* a body, but that it *is* the Body of Christ. "We, who are many, are one body in Christ, and severally members one of another." All the members together *are* one Body, for all share his life—as though he were himself distributed among his members. I was once with a group of Chinese believers who found it very hard to understand how the Body could be one when they were all separate individuals who made it up. One Sunday I was about to break the bread at the Lord's table and I asked them to look very carefully at the loaf before I broke it. Then, after it had been distributed and eaten, I pointed out that though it was inside all of them, it was still one loaf—not many. The loaf was divided, but Christ is not divided even in the sense in which that loaf was. He is still one Spirit in us, and we are all one in him.

This is the very opposite of man's condition by nature. In Adam I have the life of Adam, but that is essentially individual. There is no union, no fellowship in sin, but only self-interest and distrust of others. As I go on with the Lord I soon discover, not only that the problem of sin and of my natural strength has to be dealt with, but that there is also a further problem created by my "individual" life, the life that is sufficient in itself and does not recognize its need for, and union in, the Body. I may have got over the problems of sin and the flesh, and yet still be a confirmed individualist. I want holiness and victory and fruitfulness for myself personally and apart, albeit from the purest motives. But such an attitude ignores the Body, and so cannot provide God with satisfaction. He must deal with me therefore in this matter also, or I shall remain in conflict with his ends. God does not blame me for being an individual, but for my individual*ism*. His greatest problem is not the outward divisions and denominations that divide his Church, but our own individualistic hearts.

Yes, the Cross must do its work here, reminding me that in Christ I have died to that old life of independence which I inherited from Adam, and that in resurrection I have become not just an individual believer in Christ but a member of his Body. There is a vast difference between the two. When I see this, I shall at once have done with independence and shall seek fellowship. The life of Christ in me will gravitate to the life of Christ in others. I can no longer take an individual line. Jealousy will go. Competition will go. Private work will go. My interests, my ambitions, my preferences, all will go. It will no longer matter which of us does the work. All that will matter will be that the Body grows.

I said: "When I *see* this . . . " That is the great need: to *see* the Body of Christ as another great divine fact; to have it break in upon our spirits by heavenly revelation that "we, who are many, *are* one body in Christ." Only the Holy Spirit can bring this home to us in all its meaning, but when he does it will revolutionize our life and work.

More Than Conquerors Through Him

We only see history back to the Fall. God sees it from the beginning. There was something in God's mind *before* the Fall, and in the ages to come that thing is to be fully realized. God knew all about sin and redemption; yet in his great purpose for the Church set forth in Genesis 2, there is no view of sin. It is as though (to speak in finite terms) he leaps in thought right over the whole story of redemption and sees the Church in future eternity, having a ministry and a (future) history which is altogether apart from sin, and wholly of God. It is the Body of Christ in glory, expressing nothing of fallen man but only that which is the image of the glorified Son of man. *This* is the Church that has satisfied God's heart and has attained dominion.

In Ephesians 5 we stand within the history of redemption, and yet through grace we still have this eternal purpose of God in view as expressed in the statement that he will "present unto himself a glorious Church." But now we note that the water of life and the cleansing Word are needed to prepare the Church (now marred by the Fall) for presentation to Christ in glory. For now there are defects to be remedied and wounds to be healed. And yet how precious is the promise and how gracious are the words used of her: "not having spot"—the scars of sin, whose very history is now forgotten; "or wrinkle"—the marks of age and of time lost, for all is now made up and all is new; and "without blemish"—so that Satan or demons or men can find no grounds for blame in her.

This is where we are now. The age is closing, and Satan's power is greater than ever. Our warfare is with angels and principalities and powers (Rom. 8:38; Eph. 6:12) who are set to withstand and destroy the work of God in us by laying many things to the charge of God's elect. Alone we could never be their match, but what we alone cannot do, the Church can. Sin, self-reliance and individualism were Satan's master-strokes at the heart of God's purpose in man, and in the Cross, God has undone them. As we put our faith in what he has done—in "God that justifieth" and in "Christ Jesus that died" (Rom. 8:33–34)—we present a front against which the very gates of Hades shall not prevail. We, his Church, are "more than conquerors through him that loved us" (Rom. 8:37).

CHAPTER 12

The Cross and the Soul Life

God has made full provision for our redemption in the Cross of Christ, but he has not stopped there. In that Cross, he has also made secure beyond possibility of failure that eternal plan which Paul speaks of as having been, from all the ages "hid in God who created all things." That plan He has now proclaimed

> to the intent that now unto the principalities and the powers in the heavenly places might be made known through the church the manifold wisdom of God, according to the eternal purpose which he purposed in Christ Jesus our Lord (Eph. 3:9–11).

We have said that the work of the Cross has two results which bear directly upon the realizing of that purpose in us. On the one hand, it has issued in the release of his life that it may find expression in us through the indwelling Spirit. On the other hand, it has made possible what we speak of as "bearing the cross"; that is, our co-operation in the daily inworking of his death, whereby [a] way is made in us for the manifestation of that new life, through the bringing of the "natural man" progressively into his right place of subjection to the Holy Spirit. Clearly these are the positive and the negative sides of one thing. Equally clearly, we are now touching more particularly on the matter of progress in a life lived for God. Hitherto in dealing with the Christian life we have placed our main emphasis upon the crisis by which it is entered. Now our concern is more definitely with the walk of the disciple, having especially in view his training as a servant of God. It is of him that the Lord Jesus said: "Whosoever doth not bear his own cross, and come after me, cannot be my disciple" (Luke 14:27).

So we come to a consideration of the natural man and the "bearing of the cross." To understand this, we must, at the risk of being tedious, go back once more to Genesis and consider what it was that God sought to have in man at the beginning and how his purpose was frustrated. In this way we shall be able to grasp more clearly the principles by which we can come again to live in line with that purpose.

The True Nature of the Fall

If we have even a little revelation of the plan of God, we shall always think much of the word "man." We shall say with the Psalmist, "What is man, that thou art mindful of him?" The Bible makes it clear that what God desires above all things is a man—a man who will be after his own heart.

So God created a man. In Genesis 2:7 we learn that Adam was created *a living soul*, with a *spirit* inside to commune with God and with a *body* outside to have contact with the material world. (Such New Testament verses as 1 Thessalonians 5:23 and Hebrews 4:12 confirm this threefold character of man's being.) With his spirit, Adam was in touch with the spiritual world of God; with his body, he was in touch with the physical world of material things. He gathered up these two sides of God's creative act into himself to become a personality, an entity living in the world, moving by itself and *having powers of free choice*. Viewed thus as a whole, he was found to be a self-conscious and self-expressing being, "a living soul."

We saw earlier that Adam was created perfect—by which we mean that he was without imperfections, because [he was] created by God—but that he was not yet perfected. He needed a finishing touch somewhere. God had not yet done all that he intended to do in Adam. There was more in view, but it was as yet in abeyance. God was moving towards the fulfillment of his

148

purpose in creating man, a purpose which went beyond man himself, for it had in view the securing to God of all his rights in the universe, through man's instrumentality. But how could man be instrumental in this? Only by a co-operation that sprang from living union with God. God was seeking to have not merely a race of men of one blood upon the earth, but a race which had, in addition, his life resident within its members. Such a race will eventually compass Satan's downfall and bring to fulfillment all that God has set his heart upon. It is this that was in view with the creation of man.

Then again, we saw that Adam was created neutral. He had a spirit which enabled him to hold communion with God; but as man he was not yet, so to speak, finally orientated; he had powers of choice and he could, if he liked, turn the opposite way. God's goal in man was "sonship," or, in other words, the expression of his life in human sons. That divine life was represented in the garden by the tree of life, bearing a fruit that could be accepted, received, taken in. If Adam, created neutral, were voluntarily to turn that way and, choosing dependence upon God, were to receive of the tree of life (representing God's own life), God would then have that life in union with men; he would have secured his Spiritual sons. But if instead Adam should turn to the tree of the knowledge of good and evil, he would as a result be "free," in the sense of being able to develop himself on his own lines apart from God. Because, however, this latter choice involved complicity with Satan, Adam would thereby put beyond his reach the attaining of his God-appointed goal.

The Human Soul

Now, we know the course that Adam chose. Standing between the two trees, he yielded to Satan and took of the fruit of the tree of knowledge. This determined the lines of his development. From then on he could command a knowledge; he "knew." But—and here we come to the point—the fruit of the tree of knowledge made the first man *over-developed in his soul*. The emotion was touched, because the fruit was pleasant to the eyes, making him "desire"; the mind with its reasoning power was developed, for he was "made wise"; and the will was strengthened, so that in future he could always decide which way he would go. The whole fruit ministered to the expansion and full development of the soul, so that not only was the man a living soul, but from henceforth man will *live by the soul*. It is not merely that man *has* a soul, but that from that day on, the soul, with its independent powers of free choice, usurps the place of the spirit as the animating power of man.

We have to distinguish here between two things, for the difference is most important. God does not mind—in fact he, of course, intends—that we should have a soul such as he gave to Adam. But what God has set himself to do is to reverse something. There is something in man today which is not just the fact of *having* and *exercising* a soul, but which constitutes a *living by* the soul. It was this that Satan brought about in the Fall. He trapped man into taking a course by which he could develop his soul so as to derive from it his very spring of life.

We must, however, be careful. To remedy this does not mean that we are going to cross out the soul altogether. You cannot do that. When today the Cross is really working in us, we do not become inert, insensate, characterless. No, we still possess a soul, and whenever we receive something from God, the soul will still be used in relation to it, as an instrument, a faculty, in a true subjection to him. But the point is, are we keeping within God's appointed limit—that is to say, within the bounds set by him in the Garden at the beginning—with regard to the soul, or are we getting outside those bounds?

What God is now doing is the pruning work of the vinedresser. In our souls there is an uncontrolled development, an untimely growth, that has to be checked and dealt with. God must cut that off. So now there are two things before us to which our eyes must be opened. On the one hand, God is seeking to bring us to the place where we live by the life of his Son. On the other hand, he is doing a direct work in our hearts to undo that other natural resource that is the result of the fruit of knowledge. Every day we are learning these two lessons: a rising up of the life of this One, and a checking and a handing over to death of that other soul-life. These two processes go on all the time, for God is seeking the fully developed life of his Son in us in order to manifest himself, and to that end he is bringing us back, as to our soul, to Adam's starting-point. So Paul says: "We which live are always delivered unto death for Jesus' sake, that the life also of Jesus may be manifested in our mortal flesh" (2 Cor. 4:11).

What does this mean? It simply means that I will not take any action without relying on God. I will find no sufficiency in myself. I will not take any step just because I have the power to do so. Even though I have that inherited power within me, I will not go ahead solely upon it as basis; I will put no reliance in myself. By taking the fruit, Adam became possessed of an inherent power to act, but a power which, by its independence of God, played right into Satan's hands. You lose that power to act when you come to know the Lord. The Lord cuts it off, and you find you can no longer act on your own initiative. You have to live by the life of Another; you have to draw everything from him.

Oh, friends, I think we all know ourselves in measure, but many a time we do not truly tremble at ourselves. We may, in a manner of courtesy to God, say: "If the Lord does not want it, I cannot do it," but in reality our subconscious thought is that really we can do it quite well ourselves, even if God does not ask us to do it nor empower us for it. Too often we have been caused to act, to think, to decide, to have power, regardless of Him. Many of us Christians today are men with over-developed souls. We have grown too big in ourselves. When we are in that condition, it is possible for the life of the Son of God in us to be confined and crowded almost out of action.

Natural Energy in the Work of God

The power, the energy of the soul is present with us all. Those who have been taught by the Lord repudiate that principle as a life principle; they refuse to live by it; they will not let it reign, nor allow it to be the power-spring of the work of God. But those who have not been taught of God rely upon it; they utilize it; they think it is *the* power.

Let us take first an obvious illustration of this. Far too many of us in the past have reasoned as follows. Here is a delightfully good-natured man, with a clear brain, splendid managing powers, and sound judgment. In our hearts we say, "If that man could be a Christian, what an asset he would be to the Church! If only he were the Lord's, what a lot it would mean to His cause!"

But think for a moment. Where did that man's good nature come from? Whence are those splendid managing powers and that good judgment? Not from new birth, for he is not yet born again. We know we have all been born of the flesh; therefore we need a new birth. But the Lord Jesus had something to say about this in John 3:6: "That which is born of the flesh is flesh." Everything which comes not by new birth but my natural birth, is flesh and will only bring glory to man, not God. That statement is not very palatable, but it is true.

We have spoken of soul-power or natural energy. What is this natural energy? It is simply what *I* can do, what *I* am of myself, what *I* have inherited of natural gifts and resources. We are none of us without the power of the soul, and our first need is to recognize it for what it is.

Take for example the human mind. I may have by nature a keen mind. Before my new birth I had it naturally, as something developed from my natural birth. But the trouble arises here. I become converted, I am born anew, a deep work is effected in my spirit, and essential union has been wrought with the Father of our Spirits. Thereafter, there are in me two things: I have now a union with God that has been set up in my spirit, but at the same time I carry over with me something which I derive from my natural birth. Now what am I going to do about it?

The natural tendency is this. Formerly I used to use my mind to pore over history, over business, over chemistry, over questions of the world, or literature, or poetry. I used my keen mind to get the best out of those studies. But now my desire has been changed, so henceforth I employ the same mind in just the same way in the things of God. *I have therefore changed my subject of interest, but I have not changed my method of working.* That is the whole point. My interests have been utterly changed (praise God for that!), but now I utilize the same power to study Corinthians and Ephesians that I used before to pursue history and geography. But that power is not of the new creation; and God will not be satisfied with this simple exchange of interests. The trouble with so many of us is that we have changed the channel into which our energies are directed, but we have not changed the source of those energies.

You will find there are many such things which we carry over into the service of God. Consider the matter of eloquence. There are some men who are born orators; they can present a case very convincingly indeed. Then they become converted, and, without asking ourselves where they really stand in relation to spiritual things, we put them on the platform and make preachers of them. We encourage them to use their natural powers for preaching, and again it is a change of subject but the same power. We forget that, in the matter of our resource for handling the things of God, it is a question not of comparative value but of *origin*—of where the resource springs from. It is not so much a matter of what we are doing, but of what powers we are employing to do it, and who is controlling those powers. The man God can use may well be eloquent, but there is the mark of the Cross upon that eloquence, and the controlling hand of the Spirit of God is apparent in its use. We think too little of the source of our energy and too much of the end to which it is directed, forgetting that, with God the end never justifies the means.

To test the truth of this, let us take a hypothetical case. Mr. A. is a very good speaker: he can talk fluently and most convincingly on any subject, but in practical things he is a very bad manager. Mr. B., on the other hand, is a poor speaker: he cannot express himself clearly but wanders all round his subject, never coming to a point; yet on the other hand he is a splendid manager, most competent in all matters of business. Both these men get converted, and both become earnest Christians. Let us suppose now that I call on them both and ask them to speak at a convention, and that both accept.

Now what will happen? I have asked the self-same thing of both men, but who do you think will pray the harder? Almost certainly Mr. B. Why? Because he is no speaker. In the matter of eloquence he has no resources of his own to depend upon. He will pray: "Lord, if you do not give me power for this, I cannot do it." Of course Mr. A. will pray too, but maybe not in the same way as Mr. B., because he has something of natural aptitude upon which to rely.

Now let us suppose that, instead of asking them to speak, I ask them both to take charge of the practical side of affairs at the convention. What will happen? The position will be exactly reversed. Now it will be Mr. A.'s turn to pray hard, for he knows full well that he has no organizing ability. Mr. B, of course, will pray too, but perhaps without quite the same urgency, for though he knows his need of the Lord, he is not nearly so conscious of his need in business matters as is Mr. A.

Do you see the difference between natural and spiritual gifts? Anything we can do without prayer and without an utter dependence upon God must come from that spring of *natural* life that is tainted with the flesh. We must see this clearly. Of course it is not true that those only are suited for a particular work who lack the natural gift for it. The point is that, whether naturally gifted or not—and we should praise God for all his gifts—they must know

153

the touch of the Cross in death upon all that is of nature, and their complete dependence upon the God of resurrection. All too readily do we envy our neighbor who has some outstanding natural gift, and fail to realize that our own possession of it, apart from such a working of the Cross, could prove a barrier to the very thing that God is seeking to manifest in us.

Shortly after my conversion I went out preaching in the villages. I had had a good education and was well versed in the Scriptures, so I considered myself thoroughly capable of instructing the village folk, among whom were quite a number of illiterate women. But after several visits I discovered that, despite their illiteracy, those women hand an intimate knowledge of the Lord. I knew the Book they haltingly read; they knew the One of whom the Book spoke. I had much *in myself*; they had much *in the Spirit.* How many Christian teachers today are teaching others as I was then, very largely in the strength of their carnal equipment!

Once I met a young brother—young, that is to say, in years, but who had learned a good deal of the Lord. God had brought him through much tribulation to gain that knowledge of himself. As I was talking with him I said, "Brother, what has the Lord really been teaching you these days?"

He replied, "Only one thing: that I can do nothing apart from him."

"Do you really mean," I asked, "that you can do *nothing?*"

"Well, no," he said. "I *can* do many things! In fact that has been just my trouble. Oh, you know, I have always been so confident in myself. I know I am well able to do lots of things."

So I asked, "What then do you mean when you say you can do nothing apart from Him?"

He answered, "The Lord has shown me that I *can* do anything, but that *he* has said, 'Apart from me ye can do nothing.' So it comes to this, that everything I have done and can do apart from him *is nothing!*"

We have to come to that valuation. I do not mean to say we cannot do a lot of things, for we can. We can take meetings, and build churches, we can go to the ends of the earth and found missions, and we can seem to bear fruit; but remember that the Lord's word is: "Every plant which my heavenly Father planted not, shall be rooted up" (Matt. 15:13). God is the only legitimate Originator in the universe (Gen. 1:1), and his Holy Spirit is the only legitimate initiator in our hearts. Anything that you or I plan and set on foot with Him has the taint of the flesh upon it, and it will never reach the realm of the Spirit, however earnestly we seek God's blessing on it. It may last for years, and then we may think we will adjust here and improve there and maybe bring it on a better plane, but it cannot be done.

Origin determines destination, and what was "of the flesh" originally will never be made spiritual by any amount of "improvement." That which is born of the flesh is flesh, and it will never be otherwise. Anything for which we are sufficient in ourselves is "nothing" in God's estimate, and we have to accept his estimate and write it down as nothing. "The flesh profiteth nothing." It is only what comes from above that will abide.

We cannot see this simply by being told it. God must teach us what is meant, by putting his finger on something which he sees and saying: "This is natural; this has its source in the old creation, and did not originate with Me; this cannot abide." Until he does so, we may agree in principle, but we can never really *see* it. We may assent to, and even enjoy, the teaching, but we shall never truly loathe ourselves.

But there will come a day when God opens our eyes. Facing a particular issue we shall have to say, as by revelation: "It is unclean, it is impure; Lord, I see it!" The word "purity" is a blessed word. I always associate it with the Spirit. Purity means something altogether of the Spirit. Impurity means *mixture*. When God opens our eyes to see that the natural life is something, in itself, he can never use in his work, then we find we do not *enjoy* the doctrine any longer. Rather we loathe ourselves for the impurity that is in us; but when that point is reached, God begins his work of deliverance. We are going on shortly to look at the provision he has made for that deliverance, but we must stay for a little longer with this matter of revelation.

The Light of God and Knowledge

Of course, if one does not set out to serve the Lord whole-heartedly, one does not feel the necessity for light. It is only when one has been apprehended by God, and seeks to go forward with him, that one finds how necessary light is. There is a fundamental need for light in order for us to know the mind of God; to know what is of the spirit and what is of the soul; to know what is divine and what is merely of man; to discern what is truly heavenly and what is only earthly; to understand the difference between things which are spiritual and things which are carnal; to know whether God is really leading us, or whether we are just being moved by our feelings, senses, or imaginations. It is when we have reached a position where we would like to follow God fully that we find light to be the most necessary thing in the Christian life.

In my conversations with younger brothers and sisters, one question comes up again and again. It is: "How can I know that I am walking in the Spirit? How do I distinguish which prompting within me is from the Holy Spirit and which is from myself?" It seems that all are alike in this; but some have gone further. They are trying to look within, to differentiate, to discriminate to analyze, and in doing so are bringing themselves into deeper bondage. Now this is a situation which is really dangerous to Christian life, for inward knowledge will never be reached along the barren path of self-analysis.

We are never told in the Word of God to examine our inward condition.[1] That way ends only to uncertainty, vacillation, and despair. Of course we have to have self-knowledge. We have to know what is going on within. We do not want to live in a fool's paradise; to have gone altogether wrong and yet not know we have gone wrong; to have a spartan will and yet think we are pursuing the will of God. But such self-knowledge does not come by our turning within; by our analyzing our feelings and motives and everything that is going on inside, and then trying to pronounce whether we are walking in the flesh or in the Spirit.

There are several passages in the Psalms which illumine this subject. The first is in Psalm 36:9: "In thy light, shall we see light." I think that is one of the best verses in the old Testament. There are two lights there. There is "thy light," and then, when we have come into that light, we shall "see light."

Now those two lights are different. We might say that the first is objective and the second subjective. The first light is the light which belongs

---

[1] The two apparent exceptions to this are found in 1 Corinthians 11:28, 31 and 2 Corinthians 13:5. But the former passage calls upon us to discern ourselves as to whether we recognize the Lord's body or not, and this is in particular connection with the Lord's table. It is not concerned with self-knowledge as such. The strong command of Paul in the latter passage is to examine ourselves as to whether or not we are "in the faith." It is a question of the existence or otherwise in us of a fundamental faith; of whether, in fact, we are Christians. This is in no way related to our daily walk in the Spirit, or to self-knowledge.—*Watchman Nee*

to God but is shed upon us; the second is the knowledge imparted by that light. "In thy light shall we see light": we shall know something; we shall be clear about something; we shall *see*. No turning within, no introspective self-examination will ever bring us to that clear place. No, it is when there is light coming from God that we see.

I think it is so simple. If we want to satisfy ourselves that our face is clean, what do we do? Do we feel it carefully all over with our hands? No, of course not. We find a mirror and we bring it to the light. In that light everything becomes clear. No sight ever came by feeling or analyzing. Sight only comes by the light of God coming in; and when once it has come, there is no longer need to ask if a thing is right or wrong. We know.

You remember again how in Psalm 139:23 the writer says: "Search me, O God, and know my heart." You realize, do you not, what it means to say "Search me"? It certainly does not mean that I search myself. "Search me" means "*You* search me!" That is the way of illumination. It is for God to come in and search; it is not for me to search. Of course that will never mean that I may go blindly on, careless of my true condition. That is not the point. The point is that, however much my self-examination may reveal in me that needs putting right, such searching never really gets below the surface. My true knowledge of self comes not from my searching myself, but from God searching me.

But, you ask, what does it mean in practice for us to come into the light? How does it work? *How* do we see light in his light? Here again the Psalmist comes to our help. "The entrance of thy words giveth light; it giveth understanding unto the simple" (Psalm 119:130 AV). In spiritual things, we are all "simple." We are dependent upon God to give us understanding, and especially is this so in the matter of our own true nature. And it is here that the Word of God operates. In the New Testament the passage which states this most clearly is in the Epistle to the Hebrews:

> The word of God is living, and active, and sharper than any two-edged sword, and piercing even to the dividing of soul and spirit, of both joints and marrow, and quick to discern the thoughts and intents of the heart. And there is no creature that is not manifest in his sight: but all things are naked and laid open before the eyes of him with whom we have to do (Heb. 4:12–13).

Yes, it is the Word of God, the penetrating Scripture of Truth, that settles our questions. It is that which discerns our motives and defines for us their true source in soul or spirit.

With this, I think we can pass on from the doctrinal to the practical side of things. Many of us, I am sure, are living quite honestly before God. We have been making progress, and we do not know of anything much wrong with us. Then one day, as we go on, we meet with a fulfillment of that word: "The entrance of thy words giveth light." Some servant of God has been used by Him to confront us with his living Word, and that Word has made an entrance into us. Or perhaps we ourselves have been waiting before God and, whether from our memory of Scripture or from the page itself, his Word has come to us in power. Then it is we see something which we have never seen before. We are convicted. We know where we are wrong, and we look up and confess:

Lord, I see it. There is impurity there. There is mixture. How blind I was! Just fancy that for so many years I have been wrong there and have never known it!

Light comes in and we see light. The light of God brings us to see the light concerning ourselves, and it is an abiding principle that every knowledge of self comes to us in that way.

It may not always be the Scriptures. Some of us have known saints who really knew the Lord, and through praying with them or talking with them, in the light of God radiating from them, we have seen something which we never saw before. I have met one such, who is now with the Lord, and I always think of her as a "lighted" Christian. If I did but walk into her room, I was brought immediately to a sense of God. In those days I was very young, and had been converted about two years, and I had lots of plans, lots of beautiful thoughts, lots of schemes for the Lord to sanction, a hundred and one things which I thought would be marvelous if they were all brought to fruition. With all these things, I came to her to try to persuade her; to tell her that this or that was the thing to do.

Before I could open my mouth, she would just say a few words in quite an ordinary way. Light dawned! It simply put me to shame. My "doing" and my scheming were all so natural, so full of man. Something happened. I was brought to a place where I could say: "Lord, my mind is set only in creaturely activities, but here is someone who is not out for them at all. Teach me to walk that way." She had but one motive, one desire, and that was for God. Written in the front of her Bible were these words: "Lord, I want nothing for myself." Yes, she lived for God alone, and where that is the case, you will find that such a one is bathed in light, and that that light illuminates others. That is real witness.[2]

Light has one law: it shines wherever it is admitted. That is the only requirement. We may shut it out of ourselves; it fears nothing else. If we throw ourselves open to God, he will reveal. The trouble comes when we have closed areas, locked and barred places in our hearts, where we think with pride that *we* are right. Our defeat then lies less in our being wrong than in our *not knowing that we are wrong*. Wrong may be a question of natural strength; ignorance of it is a question of light. You can see the natural strength in some but they cannot see it themselves. Oh, we need to be sincere and humble, and to open ourselves before God! Those who are *open* can see. God is light, and we cannot live in his light and be without understanding. Let us say again with the Psalmist: "O send out thy light and thy truth: let them lead me" (Psalm 43:3).

We praise God that today sin is being brought to the notice of Christians more than hitherto. In many places the eyes of Christians have been opened to see that victory over sin is important in Christian life, and in consequence, many are walking closer to the Lord in seeking deliverance there. Praise the Lord for any movement toward himself, any movement back to real holiness unto God! But that is not enough. There is one thing that must be touched, and that is the very life of the man, not merely his sins. The question of his soul-power, his driving force, lies still at the heart of the things. To make everything of sin, or even of the flesh in its more obvious manifestations, is still to be on the surface. You have not yet got to the root of the problem.

Adam did not let sin into the world by committing murder. That came later. Adam let in sin by choosing to have his soul developed to a place where he could go on by himself apart from God. When, therefore, God secures for

---

[2] This is one of several references by the author to the late Miss Margaret E. Barber of Pagoda Anchorage, Foochow. See also pp. 168, 181, and 188.—*Angus Kinnear* [Margaret Emma Barber (1866–1930) was a missionary in several areas of China, both sponsored by the Anglican church and without denominational connection, and wrote a number of hymns and poems that show a deep experience of God. Born in Suffolk, England, she died in Pagoda Anchorage, China.]

his glory that race of men who will be the instrument of his purpose in the universe, they will be a people whose life—yea, whose very breath—is dependent upon him. He will be the "tree of life" to them.

What I more and more feel the need of in myself, and what I believe, as His children we all need to seek from God, is a real revelation of ourselves. I repeat that I do not mean we should be forever looking within and asking: "Now, is this soul or is it spirit?" That will never get us anywhere; it is darkness. No, Scripture shows us how the saints were brought to self-knowledge. It was always by light from God, and that light *is* God himself. Isaiah, Ezekiel, Daniel, Peter, Paul, John: all came to a knowledge of themselves because the Lord flashed *himself* upon them, and that flash brought revelation and conviction. (Isa. 6:5; Ezek. 1:28; Dan. 10:8; Luke 22:61, 62; Acts 9:3–5; Rev. 1:17.)

We can never know the hatefulness of sin or the treachery of our self-nature until there is that flash of God upon us. I speak not of a sensation, but of an inward revelation of the Lord himself through his Word. Such a breaking in of divine light does for us what doctrine alone can never do.

Christ is our light. He is the living Word, and when we read the Scriptures, that life in him brings revelation. "The life was the light of men" (John 1:4). Such illumination may not come to us all at once, but gradually; but it will be more and more clear and searching, until we see ourselves in the light of God, and all our self-confidence is gone. For light is the purest thing in the world. It cleanses. It sterilizes. It kills what should not be there. In its radiance the "dividing asunder of joints and marrow" becomes to us a fact and no mere teaching. We know fear and trembling as we recognize the corruption of our nature, the hatefulness of self, and the real threat to the work of God of our soul-life and energy, untamed and uncontrolled by his Holy Spirit. As never before, we see now how much of us needs God's drastic dealing if he is to use us, and we know that, apart from his dominion, as servants of God, we are finished.

But here the Cross, in its widest meaning, will come to our help again, and we shall seek now to examine an aspect of its work which meets and deals with our problem of the human soul. For only a thorough understanding of the Cross can bring us to that place of dependence which the Lord Jesus himself voluntarily took when he said, "I can of myself do nothing: as I hear, I judge: and my judgment is righteous; because I seek not mine own will, but the will of him that sent me" (John 5:30).

CHAPTER 13

The Path of Progress: Bearing the Cross

In our previous chapter we have touched several times upon the matter of service for the Lord. As we come now to look at the provision that God has made to meet the problem created by the soul-life of man, it will be helpful if we approach that problem by considering first the principles which regulate all such service. God has laid down spiritual laws which govern our world for him, and from which no one who tries to serve him may deviate. The basis of our salvation, as we well know, is the fact of the Lord's death and resurrection; but the conditions of our service are no less definite. Just as the fact of the death and resurrection of the Lord is the ground of our acceptance with God, so the *principle* of death and resurrection is the basis of our life and service for him.

The Basis of All True Ministry

No one can be a true servant of God without knowing the principle of death and the principle of resurrection. Even the Lord Jesus himself served on that basis. You will find in Matthew 3 that, before his public

161

ministry ever began, our Lord submitted himself to baptisim. He was baptized not because he had any sin, or anything which needed cleansing. No, we know the meaning of baptism: it is a figure of death and resurrection. The ministry of the Lord did not begin until, in figure, he had taken his stand there. After he had been baptized and had voluntarily taken the ground of death and resurrection, the Holy Spirit came upon him, and then he ministered.

What does this teach us? Our Lord was a sinless man. None but he has trodden this earth and known no sin. Yet as man he had a separate personality from his Father. Now we must tread very carefully when we touch our Lord; but remember his words: "I seek not mine own will, but the will of him that sent me." What does this mean? It certainly does not mean that the Lord had no will of his own. He had a will, as his own words show. As Son of man he had a will, but he did not do it; he came to do the will of the Father. So this is the point. That element in him which is in distinction from the Father is the human soul, which he assumed when he was "found in fashion as a man." Being a perfect man, our Lord had a soul, and of course a body, just as you and I have a soul and a body, and it was possible for him to act *from the soul*—that is, from himself.

You remember that immediately after the Lord's baptism, and before his public ministry began, Satan came and tempted him. He tempted him to satisfy his essential needs by turning stones to bread; to secure immediate respect for his ministry by appearing miraculously in the temple court; and to assume without delay the world dominion destined for him—and you are inclined to wonder why he tempted him to do such strange things. He might rather, you feel, have tempted him to sin in a more thoroughgoing way. But Satan did not; he knew better. He only said: "*If thou art the Son of God,* command that these stones become bread." What did it mean? The implication was this:

> If you are the Son of God, you must do something to prove it. Here is a challenge. Some will certainly raise a question as to whether your claim is real or not. Why do you not settle the matter finally now by coming out and proving it?

The whole subtle object of Satan was to get the Lord to act for himself—that is, from the soul—and, by the stand he took, the Lord Jesus absolutely repudiated such action. In Adam, man had acted from himself apart from God; that was the whole tragedy of the garden. Now in a similar situation the Son of Man takes another ground. Later he defines it as his basic life-principle—and I like the word in the Greek: "The Son can do nothing *out from* himself" (John 5:19). That total denial of the soul-life was to govern all his ministry.

So we can safely say that all the work which the Lord Jesus did on earth, prior to his actual death on the cross, was done with the principle of death and resurrection as basis, even though as an actual event Calvary still lay in the future. Everything he did was on that ground. But if this is so—if the Son of man has to go through death and resurrection (in figure and in principle) in order to work, can we do otherwise? Surely no servant of the Lord can serve him without himself knowing the working of that principle in his life. It is, of course, out of the question.

Jesus made this very clear to his disciples when he left them. He had died and was risen, and now he told them to wait in Jerusalem for power to come upon them. Now what is this power of the Holy Spirit, this "power from on high" of which he spoke? It is nothing less than the virtue of his death, resurrection, and ascension. To use another figure, the Holy Spirit is the Vessel in whom all the values of the death, resurrection, and exaltation of the Lord are deposited, that they may be brought to us. He is the one who "contains" those values and mediates them to men. That is why the Spirit could not be given before Jesus had been glorified. Then only could he rest upon men and women that they might witness; for without the values of the death and resurrection of Christ, all such witness is empty.

If we turn to the Old Testament we find the same thing is there. I would refer you to a familiar passage in the seventeenth chapter of Numbers. The matter of Aaron's ministry has been contested. There is a question among the people as to whether Aaron is truly the chosen of God. They have entertained a suspicion, and have said in effect: "Whether that man is ordained of God or not, we do not know!" and so God sets out to prove who is his servant and who is not. How does he do so? Twelve dead rods are laid before the Lord in the sanctuary over against the testimony, and are left there for a night. Then, in the morning, the Lord indicates his chosen minister by the rod which buds, blossoms and bears fruit.

We all know the meaning of that. The budding rod speaks of resurrection. It is death and resurrection that marks God-recognized ministry. Without that you have nothing. The budding of Aaron's rod proved him to be on a true basis, and God will only recognize as his ministers those who have come through death to resurrection ground.

We have seen the death of Christ working in different ways. We know how it has worked in regard to the forgiveness of our sins, and that without the shedding of Blood there is no remission. Further on, we have seen how his death works to deliver us from sin's power, and our old man has been crucified with him, in order that henceforth we should not serve sin. Going further still, the question of human self-will arose, and our need of consecration became apparent; and we found death working that way to bring about in us a willingness to let go our own choices and obey him. That indeed constitutes a starting-point for our ministry, but still it does not touch the core of the question. There may still be the lack of knowledge of what is meant by the soul.

Then another phase is presented to us in Romans 7, where the question of holiness of life is in view—a living, personal holiness. There you find a true man of God trying to please God in righteousness, and he comes under the law, and the law finds him out. He is trying to please God by using his own carnal power, and the Cross has to bring him to the place where he says, "I cannot do it. I cannot satisfy God with *my* powers; I can only trust the Holy Spirit to do that in me." I believe some of us have passed through deep waters to learn this, and to discover the value of the death of the Lord working in this way.

Now mark you, there is still a great difference between "the flesh," as spoken of in Romans 7 in relation to holiness of life, and the working of the natural energies of the soul-life in the service of the Lord. With all the above being known—and known in experience—there still remains this one sphere more which the death of the Lord must enter before we are truly of service to him. Even with all these experiences, we are still unsafe for him to use until this further thing is effected in us. How many of God's servants are used by him, as we say in China, to build twelve feet of wall, only, when they have done so, to undo it all by themselves pulling down fifteen feet! We are used in a sense, but at the same time we destroy our own work, and sometimes that of others also, because of there being some-where, something undealt with by the Cross.

Now we have to see how the Lord has set out to deal with the soul, and then more particularly how this touches the question of our service for him.

The Subjective Working of the Cross

We must keep before us now four passages from the Gospels. They are: Matthew 10:34–39; Mark 8:32–35; Luke 17:32–34; and John 12:24–26. These four passages have something in common. In each you have the Lord himself speaking to us concerning the soul-activity of man, and in each a dif-ferent aspect or manifestation of the soul-life is touched upon. In these verses he makes it very plain that the soul of man can be dealt with in one way and in one way only, and that is by our bearing the cross daily and following him.

As we have just seen, the soul-life or natural life that is here in view is something further than what we have in those passages which are con-cerned with the old man or the flesh. We have sought to make quite clear that, in respect of our old man, God emphasizes the thing he has done *once for all* in crucifying us with Christ on the Cross. We have seen that three times in the Epistle to the Galatians, the "crucifying" aspect of the Cross is referred to as a thing accomplished; and in Romans 6:6 we have the clear statement that "our old man was crucified," which, if the tense of the word means anything, we might well paraphrase: "Our old man has been finally and forever crucified." It is something *done,* to be apprehended by divine revelation and then accepted by an act of simple faith.

But there is a further aspect of the Cross, namely, that implied in the ex-pression "bearing his cross daily," which is before us now. The Cross has borne me; now I must bear it; and this bearing of the Cross is an inward thing. It is this that we mean when we speak of "the subjective working of the Cross." Moreover it is a continuous process; it is a step by step following after him. It is this which is now brought before us in relation to the soul, and, as we have just said, with an emphasis here that is not quite the same as with the old man. We do not have here the "crucifixion" of the soul itself, in the sense that our natural gifts and faculties, our personality and our individual-ity, are to be put away altogether. Were it so, it could hardly be said of us, as it is in Hebrews 10:39, that we are to "have faith unto the saving of the soul." (Compare 1 Peter 1:9; Luke 21:19.) No, we do not lose our souls in this sense, for to do so would be to lose our individual existence completely. The soul is still there with its natural endowments, but the Cross is brought to bear upon it to bring those natural endowments into death—to put the mark of his death upon them—and thereafter, as God may please, to give them back to us in glorious resurrection.

It is in this sense that Paul, writing to the Philippians, expresses the desire "that I may know him, and the power of his resurrection, and the fellowship of his sufferings, becoming conformed unto his death" (Phil. 3:10). The mark of death is upon the soul all the time, to bring it to the place where it is always subordinate to the Spirit and never independently asserts itself. Only the Cross, working in such a way, could make a man of the caliber of Paul, and with the natural resources hinted at in Philippians 3, so distrust his own natural strength that he could write to the Corinthians:

> I determined not to know anything among you, save Jesus Christ, and him crucified. And I was with you in weakness, and in fear, and in much trembling. And my speech and my preaching were not in persuasive words of wisdom, but in demonstration of the Spirit and of power: that your faith should not stand in the wisdom of men, but in the power of God (1 Cor. 2:2–3).

The soul is the seat of the affections, and what a great part of our decisions and actions is influenced by these! There is nothing deliberately sinful about them, mind you. It is just that there is something in us which can go out in natural affection to another person, and which, ungoverned by the Spirit, can influence wrongly our whole course of action. So in the first of the four passages before us, the Lord has to say:

> He that loveth father or mother more than me is not worthy of me; and he that loveth son or daughter more than me is not worthy of me. And he that doth not take his cross and follow after me, is not worthy of me (Matt. 10:37–38).

You note that to follow the Lord in the way of the Cross is set before us as his normal, his only way for us. What immediately follows? "He that findeth his soul shall lose it; and he that loseth his soul for my sake shall find it" (Matt. 10:39, marg.).

The secret danger lies in that subtle working of the affections to turn us away from the pathway of God; and the key to the matter is the soul. The Cross has to touch that. I have to "lose" my soul in the sense in which the Lord meant those words, and which we are seeking here to explain.

Some of us know well what it means to lose our soul. We can no longer lightly fulfill its desire; we cannot give in to it; we cannot gratify it: that is the "loss" of the soul. We are going through a painful process to discourage what the soul is asking for. And many a time we have to confess that it is not any definite sin that is keeping us from following the Lord to the end. We are held up because of some secret love somewhere, some perfectly natural affection diverting our course. Yes, human affection plays a great part in our lives, and the Cross has to come in there and do its purifying work.

Then we pass to the verses in Mark chapter 8. I think that is a most important passage. Our Lord had just taught his disciples at Caesarea Philippi that he was going to suffer death at the hands of the elders of the Jews, and then Peter, with all his love for his Master, came up and protested, saying: "Lord, do not do it; pity thyself: this shall never come to thee!" Out of his love for the Lord, he appealed to him to spare himself; and the Lord had to rebuke Peter, as he would rebuke Satan, for caring for the things of men and not the things of God. And then, to the multitude that gathered to him, the word was spoken once more:

> If any man would come after me, let him deny himself, and take up his cross, and follow me. For whosoever will save his soul shall lose it; and whosoever shall lose his soul for my sake and the gospel's shall save it (Mark 8:34–35, marg.).

The whole question at issue is again that of the soul, and here it is particularly of the soul's desire for self-preservation. There is that subtle suggestion which says, "If I could be allowed to live, I would do anything, be willing for anything; but I must be kept alive!" There you have the soul almost crying out for help.

> Going to the Cross, being crucified—oh that is really too much! Have mercy on yourself; pity yourself! Do you mean to say you are going *against yourself* and going *with God*?

167

Some of us know well that in order to go on with God, we have many a time to go against the voice of the soul—our own or other people's—and to let the Cross come in, to silence that appeal for self-preservation.

Am I afraid of the will of God? The dear saint whom I have already mentioned as having had such an influence upon the course of my life, many times asked me the question: "Do you like the will of God?" It is a tremendous question. She did not ask, "Do you *do* the will of God?": she always asked, "Do you *like* the will of God?" That question cuts deeper than anything else. I remember once she was having a controversy with the Lord over a certain matter. She knew what the Lord wanted, and in her heart she wanted it too. But is was difficult, and I heard her pray like this: "Lord, I confess I don't like it, but please do not give in to me. Just wait, Lord—and *I* will give in to thee." She did not want the Lord to yield to her and to reduce his demands upon her. She wanted nothing but to please him.

Many a time we have to come to the place where we are willing to let go to Him things we think to be good and precious—yes, and even, it may be, the very things of God themselves—that his will may be done. Peter's concern was for his Lord and was dictated by his natural love for him. We might feel that Peter had a marvelous love for his Lord, sufficient even for him to dare to question Jesus. Only a strong love could bring one to attempt that! Yes, we think we understand Peter, but when there is purity of spirit without that mixture of soul, we shall not be so readily led into Peter's mistake. We shall more quickly recognize where the will of God lies, and shall discover there, and there alone, our heart's true delight.

Once again the Lord Jesus deals with the matter of the soul, in Luke chapter 17, and now it is in relation to his return. Speaking of "the day that the Son of man is revealed," he draws a parallel between that day and "the day that Lot went out from Sodom" (verses 29–30). A little later he speaks of the "rapture" of the saints in the twice repeated words: "One shall be taken, and the other shall be left" (verses 34–35). But between his reference to the calling of Lot out of Sodom and this allusion to the gathering of the saints to him, there come these remarkable words:

> In that day, he which shall be on the housetop, and his goods in the house, let him not go down to take them away: and let him that is in the field likewise not return back. Remember Lot's wife (verses 31–32).

Remember Lot's wife! Why? Because "whosoever shall seek to gain his soul shall lose it: but whosoever shall lose his soul shall save it alive" (verse 33, marg.).

If I mistake not, this is the one passage in the New Testament that tells of our reaction to the rapture call. We may have thought that when the Son of man comes we shall be gathered to him automatically, as it were, because of what we read in 1 Corinthians 15:51–52: "We shall all be changed, in a moment, in the twinkling of an eye, at the last trump . . . " Well, however we reconcile the two passages, this one in Luke's Gospel should at least make us pause and reflect; for the emphasis is here very strongly upon one being taken and the other left. It is a matter of our reaction to the call to go, and on the basis of this a most urgent appeal is made to us to be ready (compare Matt. 24:42).

There is surely a reason for this. Clearly that call is not going to produce a miraculous last-minute change in us out of all relation to our previous walk with the Lord. No, in that moment we shall discover our heart's real treasure. If it is the Lord himself, then there will be no backward look. A backward glance decides everything. It is so easy to become more attached to the gifts of God than to the Giver—and even, I should add, to the *work* of God than to God himself.

Let me illustrate. At the present time[1] I am writing a book. I have finished eight chapters and I have another nine to write, about which I am very seriously exercised before the Lord. But if the call to "come up hither" should come and my reaction were to be "What about my book?" the answer might well be, "All right, stay down and finish it!" That precious thing which we are doing downstairs "in the house" can be enough to pin us down, a peg that holds us to earth.

It is all a question of our living by the soul or by the spirit. Here in this passage in Luke, we have depicted the soul-life in its engagement with the things of earth—and mark you, not sinful things either. The Lord only mentioned marrying, planting, eating, selling—all perfectly legitimate activities with which there is nothing essentially wrong. But it is occupation with them, so that your heart goes out to them, that is enough to pin you

---

[1] 1938.—*Angus Kinnear*

down. The way out of that danger is by the losing of the soul. This is beautifully illustrated in the action of Peter when he recognized the risen Lord Jesus by the lake-side. Though, with the others, he was back for the moment in his former employment, there was now no thought of the ship, nor even of the net full of fishes so miraculously provided. When he heard John's cry of recognition: "it is the Lord," we read that "he cast himself into the sea" to go to Jesus.

That is true detachment. The question at issue is always, "Where is my heart?" The cross has to work in us a true detachment in spirit from anything and anyone outside of the Lord himself.

But, even here, we are as yet only dealing with the more outward aspects of the soul's activity. The soul giving reign to its affections, the soul asserting itself and trying to manipulate things, the soul becoming preoccupied with things, on the earth: these are still small things, and do not yet touch the real heart of the matter. There is something deeper yet, which I will try now to explain.

The Cross and Fruitfulness

Let us read again John 12:24–25.

> Verily, verily, I say unto you, "Except a grain of wheat fall into the earth and die, it abideth by itself alone; but if it die, it beareth much fruit." He that loveth his life (Greek "soul," as in the above passages) loseth it; and he that hateth his life ("soul") in this world shall keep it unto life eternal.

Here we have the inward working of the Cross of which we have been speaking—the losing of the soul—linked with and likened to that aspect of the death of the Lord Jesus himself which we have already seen depicted in the grain of wheat, namely, his death with a view to increase. The end in view is fruitfulness. There is a grain of wheat with life in it, but "it abideth alone." It has the power to impart its life to others; but to do so it must go down into death.

Now, we know the way the Lord Jesus took. He passed into death, and, as we saw earlier, his life emerged in many lives. The Son died, and came forth as the first of "many sons." He let go his life that we might receive it. It is in this aspect of his death that we are called to die. It is here that he makes clear the value of conformity to his death, whereby we lose our own natural life in order that, in the power of his resurrection, we may become life-imparters, sharing thereafter with others the new life of God which is in us. This is the secret of ministry, the path of real fruitfulness to God. As Paul says:

> We which live are always delivered unto death for Jesus' sake, that the life of Jesus may be manifested in our mortal flesh. So then death worketh in us, but life in you (2 Cor. 4:11–12).

We are coming to our point. In us who have received Christ, there is a new life. We all have that precious possession, the treasure in the vessel. Praise the Lord for the reality of life within! But why is there so little expression of that life? Why is there an "abiding alone"? Why is it not overflowing and imparting life to others? Why is it scarcely making itself apparent even in our own lives? The reason why there is so little sign of life where life is present, is that the soul in us is enveloping and confining that life (as the husk envelopes the grain of wheat) so that it cannot find outlet. We are living in the soul; we are working and serving in our own natural strength; we are not drawing from God. It is the *soul* that stands in the way of the springing up of life. Lose it; for that way lies fullness.

A Dark Night—a Resurrection Morn

So we come back to the almond rod, which was brought into the sanctuary for a night—a dark night in which there was nothing to be seen—and then in the morning it budded. There you have set forth the death and resurrection, the life yielded up and the life gained, and there you have the ministry attested. But how does this work out in practice? How do I recognize that God is dealing with me in this way?

First we must be clear about one thing: the soul with its fund of natural energy and resource will continue with us until our death. Till then there will be an unending day-by-day need for the Cross to operate in us, dredging deeply that well-spring of nature. This is the life-long condition of service laid down by Jesus in the words: "Let him deny himself, and take up his cross, and follow me" (Mark 8:34). We never get past that. He who evades it "is not worthy of me" (Matt. 10:38); he "cannot be my disciple" (Luke 14:27). Death and resurrection must remain an abiding principle of our lives for the losing of the soul and the uprising of the Spirit of life.

171

Yet here too there may be a crisis that, once reached and passed, can transform our whole life and service for God. It is a wicket gate by which we may enter upon an entirely new pathway. Such a crisis occurred in the life of Jacob at Peniel. It was the "natural man" in Jacob that was seeking to attain God's end. Jacob knew well that God had said: "The elder shall serve the younger," but he was trying to compass that end through his own ingenuity. God had to cripple that strength of nature in Jacob, and he did so when he touched the sinew of Jacob's thigh. Jacob continued to walk thereafter, but he continued to be lame. He was a different Jacob, as his change of name implies. He had his feet and he could use them, but the strength had been touched, and he limped from an injury from which he would never quite recover.

God must bring us to a point—I cannot tell you how it will be, but he will do it—where, through a deep and dark experience, our natural power is touched and fundamentally weakened, so that we no longer dare trust ourselves. He has had to deal with some of us very harshly, and take us through difficult and painful ways, in order to get us there. At length there comes a time when we no longer "like" to do Christian work—indeed we almost dread to do things in the Lord's Name. But then at last it is that he can begin to use us.

I can tell you this, that for a year after I was converted, I had a lust to preach. It was impossible for me to stay silent. It was as though there was something moving within me that drove me forward, and I had to keep going. Preaching had become my very life. The Lord may graciously allow you to go on for a long while like that, and to do so with a fair measure of blessing, until one day that natural force impelling you is touched, and from then on, you no longer do it because you want to do it but because the Lord wants it. Before that experience, you preached for the sake of the satisfaction you got from serving God in that way; and yet sometimes the Lord could not move you to do one thing that he wanted done. You were living by the natural life, and that life varies a great deal. It is the slave of your temperament. When emotionally you are set on his way, you go ahead at full speed, but when your emotions are directed the other way, you are reluctant to move at all, even when duty calls. You are not pliable in the Lord's hands. He has therefore to weaken that strength of preference, of like and dislike, in you, until you will do a thing because he wants it, and not because you like it. You may enjoy it or you may not, but you will do it just the same. It is not that you can derive a certain satisfaction from preaching or from doing this or that work for God, and therefore you do it. No, you do it now because it is the will of God, and regardless of whether or not it gives you conscious joy. The true joy you know in doing his will lies deeper than your fluctuating emotions.

God is bringing you to the place where he has but to express a wish and you respond instantly. That is the spirit of the Servant (Psalm 40:7–8), but such a spirit does not come *naturally* to any of us. It comes only when our soul, the seat of our natural energy and will and affections, has been brought, by the touch of the Cross, under his sway. Yet such a servant-spirit is what he seeks and will have in us all. The way to it may be long-drawn, or it may be just one stroke; but God has his ways and we must have regard to them.

Every true servant of God must know at some time that disabling from which he can never recover; he can never be quite the same again. There must be that established in you which means that from henceforth you will *really* fear yourself. You will fear to move out on the impulse of your soul, for you know what a bad time you will have in your own heart before the Lord if you do. You have known something of the chastening hand of a loving God upon you, a God who "dealeth with you as with sons" (Heb. 12:7). The Spirit himself bears witness in your spirit to that relationship, and to the inheritance and glory that are ours "if so be that we suffer with him" (Rom. 8:16–17); and your response to the "Father of our spirits" is: "Abba, Father."

But when this is really established in you, you have come to a new place which we speak of as "resurrection ground." Death in principle may have had to be wrought out to a crisis in your natural life, but when it has, then you find God releases you into resurrection. You discover that what you have lost is being given back—though not quite as before. The principle of life is at work in you now: something that directs and empowers you, animating you with fresh divine life. From henceforth, what you have lost will be brought back, but touched now with new values because under heaven's control.

Let me again make this quite clear. If we want to be spiritual people, there is no need for us to amputate our hands or feet; we can still have our body. In the same way we can have our soul, with the full use of its faculties; and yet the soul is not now our life-spring. We are no longer living in it, we are no longer drawing from it and living by it; we use it. When the body becomes our life, we live like beasts. When the soul becomes our life, we live as rebels and fugitives from God—gifted, cultured, [and] educated, no doubt, but alienated from the life of God. But when we come to live our life in the Spirit, and by the Spirit, though we still use our soul faculties just as we do our physical faculties, *they are now the servants of the Spirit;* and when we have reached that point God can really use us.

But the difficulty with many of us is that dark night. The Lord graciously laid me aside once in my life for a number of months and put me, spiritually, into utter darkness. It was almost as though he had forsaken me—almost as though nothing was going on and I had really come to the end of everything. And then by degrees he brought things back again. The temptation is always to try to help God by taking things back ourselves; but remember, there must be a full night in the sanctuary—a full night in darkness. It cannot be hurried; he knows what he is doing.

We would like to have death and resurrection put together within one hour of each other. We cannot face the thought that God will keep us aside for so long a time; we cannot bear to wait. And of course I cannot tell you how long he will take, but in principle I think it is quite safe to say this, that there will be a definite period when he will keep you there. It will seem as though nothing is happening; as though everything you valued is slipping from your grasp. There confronts you a blank wall with no door in it. Seemingly everyone else is being blessed and used, while you yourself have been passed by and are losing out. Lie quiet. All is in darkness, but it is only for a night. It must indeed be a full night, but that is all. Afterwards you will find that everything is given back to you in glorious resurrection; and nothing can measure the difference between what was before and what now is!

I was sitting one day at supper with a young brother to whom the Lord had been speaking on this very question of our natural energy. He said to me, "It is a blessed thing when you know the Lord has met you and touched you in that fundamental way, and that disabling touch has been received." There was a plate of biscuits between us on the table, and I picked one up and broke it in half as though to eat it. Then, fitting the two pieces together again carefully, I said, "It looks all right, but it is never quite the same again, is it? When once your back is broken, you will yield ever after to the slightest touch from God."

That is it. The Lord knows what he is doing with his own, and he has left no aspect of our need unmet in his Cross, that the glory of the Son may be manifested in the sons. Disciples who have gone this way can, I believe, truly echo the words of the apostle Paul, who could claim to serve God "in my spirit in the gospel of his Son" (Rom. 1:9). They have learned, as he had, the secret of such a ministry: "We . . . worship by the Spirit of God, and glory in Christ Jesus, and have no confidence in the flesh" (Phil. 3:3).

Few can have led a more active life than Paul's. To the Romans he puts it on record that he has preached the Gospel from Jerusalem to Illyricum (Rom. 15:19) and that he is ready now to go on to Rome (1:10) and thence, if possible, to Spain (15:24, 28). Yet in all this service, embracing as it does the whole Mediterranean world, his heart is set on one object only—the uplifting of the One who has made it all possible.

> I have therefore my glorying in Christ Jesus in things pertaining to God. For I will not dare to speak of any things save those which Christ wrought through me, for the obedience of the Gentiles, by word and deed (Rom. 15:17–18).

That is spiritual service.

May God make each one of us, as truly as he was, "a bondservant of Jesus Christ."

Chapter 14

The Goal of the Gospel

For our final chapter we will take as our starting-point an incident in the Gospels that occurs under the very shadow of the Cross—an incident that, in its details, is at once historic and prophetic.

> And while he was in Bethany in the house of Simon the leper, as he sat at meat, there came a woman having an alabaster cruse [flask] of ointment of spikenard[1] very costly; and she brake the cruse, and poured it over his head . . . Jesus said . . . "Verily I say unto you, wheresoever the gospel shall be preached throughout the whole world, that also which this woman hath done shall be spoken of for a memorial of her" (Mark 14:3, 6, 9).

Thus the Lord ordained that the story of Mary anointing him with that costly ointment should always accompany the story of the Gospel; that what Mary has done should always be coupled with what the Lord has done. That is his own statement. What does he intend that we should understand by it?

---

[1] Spikenard: a much-valued perfume

I think we all know the story of Mary's action well. From the details given in John chapter 12, where the incident follows not long after her brother's restoration to life, we may gather that the family was not a specially wealthy one. The sisters had to work in the house themselves, for we are told that at this feast "Martha also served" (John 12:2 and compare Luke 10:40).[2] No doubt every penny mattered to them. Yet one of those sisters, Mary, having among her treasures an alabaster cruse containing "three hundred pence" worth of ointment, expended the whole thing on the Lord. Human reasoning said this was really too much; it was giving the Lord more than his due. That is why Judas took the lead, and the other disciples supported him, in voicing a general complaint that Mary's action was a wasteful one.

Waste

> But there were some that had indignation among themselves, saying, "To what purpose hath this waste of the ointment been made? For this ointment might have been sold for above three hundred pence and given to the poor." And they murmured against her (Mark 14:4–5).

These words bring us to what I believe the Lord would have us consider finally together, namely, that which is signified by the little word "waste."

What is waste? Waste means, among other things, giving more than is necessary. If a shilling will do and you give a pound, it is a waste. If two grams will do and you give a kilogram, it is a waste. If three days will suffice to finish a task well enough and you lavish five days or a week on it, it is a waste. Waste means that you give something too much for something too little. If someone is receiving more than he is considered to be worth, then that is waste.

But remember, we are dealing here with something which the Lord said had to go out with the Gospel, wherever that Gospel should be carried. Why? Because he intends that the preaching of the Gospel should issue in something along the very lines of the action of Mary here, namely,

---

[2] The author here takes the fairly common view that the "house of Simon the leper" was the home of Mary, Martha and Lazarus, Simon presumably also being a relative of the two sisters.—*Angus Kinnear*

that people should come to him and waste themselves on him. This is the result that he is seeking.

We must look at this question of wasting on the Lord from two angles: that of Judas (John 12:4–6) and that of the other disciples (Matt. 26:8–9); and for our present purpose we will run together the parallel accounts.

All the twelve thought it was a waste. To Judas of course, who had never called Jesus "Lord," everything that was poured out upon him was waste. Not only was ointment waste; even water would have been waste. Here Judas stands for the world. In the world's estimation the service of the Lord, and our giving ourselves to him for such service, is sheer waste. He has never been loved, never had a place in the hearts of the world, so any giving to him is a waste. Many say: "Such-and-such a man could make good in the world if only he were not a Christian!" Because a man has some natural talent or other asset in the world's eyes, they count it a shame for him to be serving the Lord. They think such people are really too good for the Lord. "What waste of a useful life!" they say.

Let me give a personal instance. In 1929 I returned from Shanghai to my home town of Foochow. One day I was walking along the street with a stick, very weak and in broken health, and I met one of my old college professors. He took me into a teashop where we sat down. He looked at me from head to foot and from foot to head, and then he said:

> Now look here; during your college days we thought a good deal of you and we had hopes that you would achieve something great. *Do you mean to tell me that this is what you are?*

Looking at me with penetrating eyes, he asked that very pointed question. I must confess that, on hearing it, my first desire was to break down and weep. My career, my health, everything had gone, and here was my old professor who taught me law in the school, asking me: "Are you still in this condition, with no success, no progress, nothing to show?"

But the very next moment—and I have to admit that in all my life it was the first time—I really knew what it meant to have the "Spirit of glory" resting upon me. The thought of being able to pour out my life for my Lord flooded my soul with glory. Nothing short of the Spirit of glory was on me then. I could look up and without a reservation say: "Lord, I praise thee! This is the best thing possible; it is the right course that I have chosen!" To my professor it seemed a total waste to serve the Lord; but that is what the Gospel is for—to bring us to a true estimate of His worth.

Judas felt it a waste.

> We could manage better with the money by using it in some other way. There are plenty of poor people. Why not rather give it for charity, do some social service for their uplift, help the poor in some practical way? Why pour it out at the feet of Jesus? (See John 12:4–6.)

That is always the way the world reasons.

> Can you not do something better with yourself than this? It is going a bit too far to give yourself altogether to the Lord!

But if the Lord is worthy, then how can it be a waste? He is worthy to be so served. He is worthy for me to be his prisoner. He is worthy for me just to live for him. *He is worthy!* What the world says about this does not matter. The Lord says: "Do not trouble her." So let us not be troubled. Men may say what they like, but we can stand on this ground, that the Lord said: "It is a good work. Every true work is not done on the poor; every true work is done to me." When once our eyes have been opened to the real worth of our Lord Jesus, *nothing* is too good for him.

But I do not want to dwell too much on Judas. Let us go on to see what was the attitude of the other disciples, because their reaction affects us even more than does his. We do not greatly mind what the world is saying; we can stand that, but we do very much mind what other Christians are saying, who ought to understand. And yet we find that they said the same thing as Judas; and they not only said it but they were very upset, very indignant about it.

> When the disciples saw it, they had indignation, saying, "To what purpose is this waste? For this ointment might have been sold for much, and given to the poor" (Matt. 26:8–9).

Of course we know that the attitude of mind is all too common among Christians which says, "Get all you can for as little as possible." That however, is not what is in view here, but something deeper. Let me illustrate. Has someone been telling you that you are wasting your life by sitting still and not doing much? They say,

Here are people who ought to get out into this or that kind of work. They could be used to help this or that group of people. Why are they not more active?

—and in saying so, their whole idea is *use*. Everything ought to be used to the full in ways they understand.

There are those who have been very concerned with some dear servants of the Lord on this very ground, that they are apparently not *doing* enough. They could do so much more, they think, if they could secure an entry somewhere and enjoy a greater acceptance and prominence in certain circles. They could then be used in a far greater way. I have spoken already of a sister whom I knew for a long time and who, I think, is the one by whom I have been helped most. She was used of the Lord in a very real way during those years when I was associated with her, though to some of us at the time this was not so apparent. The one concern in my heart was this: "She is not used!" Constantly I said to myself,

Why does she not get out and take some meetings, go somewhere, do something? It is a waste for her to be living in that small village with nothing happening!

Sometimes, when I went to see her, I almost shouted at her. I said,

No one knows the Lord as you do. You know the Book in a most living way. Do you not see the need around? Why don't you *do* something? It is a waste of time, a waste of energy, a waste of money, a waste of everything, just sitting here and doing nothing!

But no, brethren, that is not the first thing with the Lord. He wants you and me to be used, certainly. God forbid that I should preach inactivity or seek to justify a complacent attitude to the world's need. As Jesus himself says here, "the gospel shall be preached throughout the whole world." But the question is one of emphasis. Looking back today, I realize how greatly the Lord was in fact using that dear sister to speak to a number of us who, as young men, were at that time in his training school for this very work of the Gospel. I cannot thank God enough for her and for the influence of her life upon me.

What, then, is the secret? Clearly it is this: that in approving Mary's action at Bethany, the Lord Jesus was laying down one thing as a basis of all service: that you pour out all you have, your very self, *unto him;* and if that should be all he allows you to do, that is enough. It is not first of all a question of whether "the poor" have been helped or not. That will follow, but the first question is: "Has the Lord been satisfied?"

There is many a meeting we might address, many a convention at which we might minister, many a Gospel campaign in which we might have a share. It is not that we are unable to do it. We could labor and be used to the full; but the Lord is not so concerned about our ceaseless occupation in work for him. That is not his first object. The service of the Lord is not to be measured by tangible results. No, my friends, the Lord's first concern is with our position at his feet and our anointing of his head. Whatever we have as an "alabaster box": the most precious thing, the thing dearest in the world to us—yes, let me say it, *the outflow from us of a life that is produced by the very Cross itself*—we give that all up *to the Lord.* To some, even of those who should understand, it seems a waste; but that is what he seeks above all. Often enough the giving to him will be in tireless service, but he reserves to himself the right to suspend the service for a time in order to discover to us whether it is that or himself that holds us.

Ministering to His Pleasure

Wheresoever the gospel shall be preached . . . that also which this woman hath done shall be spoken of (Mark 14:9).

Why did the Lord say this? Because the Gospel is meant to produce this. It is what the Gospel is for. The Gospel is not just to satisfy sinners. Praise the Lord, sinners will be satisfied! But their satisfaction is, we may say, a blessed by-product of the Gospel and not its primary aim. The Gospel is preached in the first place so that *the Lord* may be satisfied.

I am afraid we lay too much emphasis on the good of sinners, and we have not sufficiently appreciated what the Lord has in view as his goal. We have been thinking how the sinner will fare if there is no Gospel, but that is not the main consideration. Yes, praise God! The sinner has his part. God meets his need and showers him with blessings; but that is not the most important thing. The first thing is this, that everything should be to the satisfaction of the Son of God. It is only when he is satisfied, that we shall be satisfied, and the sinner will be satisfied. I have never met a soul who has set out to satisfy the Lord and has not been satisfied himself. It is impossible. Our satisfaction comes unfailingly when we satisfy him first.

But we have to remember this, that he will never be satisfied without our "wasting" ourselves upon him. Have you ever given too much to the Lord? May I tell you something? One lesson some of us have come to learn is this: that in divine service, the principle of waste is the principle of power. The principle which determines usefulness is the very principle of scattering. Real usefulness in the hand of God is measured in terms of "waste." The more you think you can *do,* and the more you employ your gifts up to the very limit (and some even go over the limit!) in order to do it, the more you find that you are applying the principle of the world and not of the Lord. God's ways with us are all designed to establish in us this other principle, namely, that our work *for* him springs out of our ministering *to* him. I do not mean that we are going to do nothing; but the first thing for us must be the Lord himself, not his work.

But we must come down to very practical issues. You say:

> I have given up a position; I have given up a ministry; I have foregone certain attractive possibilities of a bright future, in order to go on with the Lord in this way. Now I try to serve him. Sometimes it seems that the Lord hears me, and sometimes he keeps me waiting for a definite answer. Sometimes he uses me, but sometimes it seems that he passes me by. Then, when this is so, I compare myself with that other fellow who is in a certain big system. He too had a bright future, but he has never given it up. He continues on and he serves the Lord. He sees souls saved and the Lord blesses his ministry. He is successful—I do not mean materially, but spiritually—and I sometimes think he looks more like a Christian than I do, so happy, so satisfied. After all, what do I get out of this? He has a good time; I have all the bad time. He has never gone this way, and yet he has much that Christians today regard as spiritual prosperity, while I have all sorts of complications coming to me. What is the meaning of it all? Am I wasting my life? Have I really given too much?

So there is your problem. You feel that were you to follow in that other brother's steps—were you, shall we say, to consecrate yourself enough for the blessing but not enough for the trouble, enough for the Lord to use you but not enough for him to shut you up—all would be perfectly all right. But would it? You know quite well that it would not.

Takes your eyes off that other man! Look at your Lord, and ask yourself again what it is that he values most highly. The principle of waste is the principle that he would have govern us. "She is doing this *for Me*." Real satisfaction is brought to the heart of God only when we are really, as people would think, "wasting" ourselves upon him. It seems as though we are giving too much and getting nothing—and *that* is the secret of pleasing God.

Oh, friends, what are we seeking? Do we seek for "use", as those disciples did? They wanted to make every penny of those three hundred pence go to its full length. The whole question was one of *obvious* "usefulness" to God in terms that could be measured and put on record. The Lord waits to hear us say: "Lord, I do not mind about that. If I can only please thee, it is enough."

Anointing Him Beforehand

Let her alone; why trouble ye her? She hath wrought a good work on me. For ye have the poor always with you, and whensoever ye will ye can do them good: but me ye have not always. She hath done what she could: she hath anointed my body aforehand for the burying (Mark 14:6–8).

In these verses the Lord Jesus introduces a time-factor with the word "beforehand," and this is something of which we can have a new application today, for it is as important to us now as it was to her then. We all know that in the age to come we shall be called to a greater work—not to inactivity. "Well done, good and faithful servant: thou hast been faithful over a few things, I will set thee over many things: enter thou into the joy of thy Lord" (Matthew 25:21; and compare Matthew 24:47 and Luke 19:17). Yes, there will be a greater work; for the work of God's house will go on, just as in the story the care of the poor went on. The poor would always be with them, but they could not always have him. There was something, represented by this pouring out of the ointment, which Mary had to do *beforehand*, or she would have no later opportunity. I believe that in that day we shall all love him as we have never done now, but yet that it will be most blessed for those who have poured out their all upon the Lord today. When we see him face to face I trust that we shall all break and pour out everything for him. But *today*—what are we doing *today*?

Several days after Mary broke the alabaster box and poured the ointment on Jesus' head, there were some women who went early in the morning to anoint the body of the Lord. Did they do it? Did they succeed in their purpose on that first day of the week? No, there was only one soul who succeeded in anointing the Lord, and it was Mary, who anointed him beforehand. The others never did it, for he had risen. Now I suggest that in just such a way the matter of time may be supremely important to us also, and that the question above all questions is: "*What am I doing to the Lord* today?*"

Have our eyes been opened to see the preciousness of the One whom we are serving? Have we come to see that nothing less than the dearest, the costliest, the most precious, is fit for him? Have we recognized that working for the poor, working for the benefit of the world, working for the souls of men and for the eternal good of the sinner—all these so necessary and valuable things—are right only if they are in their place? In themselves, as things apart, they are as nothing compared with work that is done *to the Lord*.

The Lord has to open our eyes to his worth. If there is in the world some precious art treasure, and I pay the high price asked for it, be it one thousand, ten thousand, or even a fifty thousand pounds, dare anyone say it is a waste? The idea of waste only comes into our Christianity when we underestimate the worth of our Lord. The whole question is: "How precious is he to us now?" If we do not think much of him, then of course to give him anything at all, however small, will seem to us a wicked waste. But when he is really precious to our souls, nothing will be too good, nothing too costly for him; everything we have, our dearest, our most priceless treasure, we shall pour out upon him, and we shall not count it a shame to have done so.

Of Mary the Lord said: "She hath done what she could." What does that mean? It means that she had given up her all. She had kept nothing in reserve for a future day. She had lavished on him all she had; and yet on the resurrection morning she had no reason to regret her extravagance. And the Lord will not be satisfied with anything less from us, than that we too should have done "what we could." By this, remember, I do not mean the expenditure of our effort and energy in trying to do something for him, for that is not the point here. What the Lord Jesus looks for in us is a life laid at his feet—and that in view of his death and burial and of a future day. His burial was already in view that day in the home in Bethany. To-day it is his crowning that is in view—when he shall be acclaimed in glory as the Anointed One, the Christ of God. Yes, then we shall pour out our all upon him! But it is a precious thing—indeed it is a far more precious thing to him—that we should anoint him now, not with any material oil but with something costly, something from our hearts.

That which is merely external and superficial has no place here. It has already been dealt with by the Cross, and we have given our consent to God's judgment upon it and learnt to know in experience its cutting off. What God is demanding of us now is represented by that flask of alabaster: something mined from the depths, something turned and chased and wrought upon, something that, because it is so truly of the Lord, we cher-ish as Mary cherished that flask—and we would not, we dare not break it. It comes now from the heart, from the very depth of our being; and we come to the Lord with that, and we break it and pour it out and say: "Lord, here it is. It is all yours, because you are worthy!"—and the Lord has got what he desired. May he receive such an anointing from us *today*.

Fragrance

And the house was filled with the odor of the ointment (John 12:3).

By the breaking of that flask and the anointing of the Lord Jesus, the house was pervaded with the sweetest fragrance. Everyone could smell it and none could be unaware of it. What is the significance of this?

Whenever you meet someone who has really suffered—someone who has gone through experiences with the Lord that have brought limitation, and who, instead of trying to break free in order to be "used," has been willing to be imprisoned by him and has thus learned to find satisfaction in the Lord and nowhere else—then immediately you become aware of something. Immediately your spiritual senses detect a sweet savor of Christ. Something has been crushed, something has been broken in that life, and so you smell the odor. The odor that filled the house that day in Bethany still fills the Church today; Mary's fragrance never passes. It needed but one stroke to break the flask for the Lord, but her action—that unreserved giving and the fragrance of that anointing—abides.

We are speaking here of what we are; not of what we do or what we preach. Perhaps you may have been asking the Lord for a long time that he will be pleased to use you in such a way as to impart impressions of himself to others. That prayer is not exactly for the gift of preaching or teaching. It is rather that you might be able, in your touch with others, to impart God, the presence of God, the sense of God. Let me tell you, dear friends, you cannot produce such impressions of God upon others without the breaking of everything, even your most precious possessions, at the feet of the Lord Jesus.

But if once that point is reached, you may or may not seem to be much used in an outward way, but God will begin to use you to create a hunger in others. People will scent Christ in you. The most unlikely people will detect that. They will sense that here is one who has gone with the Lord, one who has suffered, one who has not moved freely, independently, but who has known what it is to subject everything to Him. That kind of life creates impressions, and impressions create hunger, and hunger provokes men to go on seeking until they are brought by divine revelation into fullness of life in Christ.

God does not set us here first of all to preach or to do work for him. The first thing for which he sets us here is to create in others a hunger for himself. That is, after all, what prepares the soil for the preaching.

If you set a delicious cake in front of two men who have just had a heavy meal, what will be their reaction? They will talk about it, admire its appearance, discuss the recipe, argue about the cost—do everything, in fact, but eat it! But if they are truly hungry it will not be very long before that cake is gone. And so it is with the things of the Spirit. No true work will ever begin in a life without first of all a sense of need being created. But how can this be done? We cannot inject spiritual appetite by force into others; we cannot compel people to be hungry. Hunger has to be created, and it can be created in others only by those who carry with them the impressions of God.

I always like to think of the words of that "great woman" of Shunem. Speaking of the prophet, whom she had observed but whom she did not know well, she said: "Behold now, I perceive that this is an holy man of God, which passeth by us continually" (2 Kings 4:9). It was not what

Elisha said or did that conveyed that impression, but what he *was*. By his merely passing by she could detect something; she could *see*. What are people sensing about us? We may leave many kinds of impressions: we may leave the impression that we are clever, that we are gifted, that *we* are this or that or the other. But no: the impression left by Elisha was an impression of God himself.

This matter of our impact upon others turns upon one thing, and that is the working of the Cross in us with regard to the pleasure of the heart of God. It demands that I seek his pleasure, that I seek to satisfy him only, and I do not mind how much it costs me to do so. The sister of whom I have spoken came once into a situation that was very difficult for her: I mean, it was costing her everything. I was with her at the time, and together we knelt down and prayed with wet eyes. Looking up she said: "Lord, I am willing to break my heart in order that I may satisfy thy heart!" To talk thus of heart-break might with many of us be merely romantic sentiment, but in the particular situation in which she was, it meant to her just that.

There must be something—a willingness to yield, a breaking and a pouring out of everything to him—which gives release to that fragrance of Christ and produces in other lives an awareness of need, drawing them out and on to know the Lord. This is what I feel to be the heart of everything. The Gospel has as its one object the producing in us sinners of a condition that will satisfy the heart of our God. In order that he may have that, we come to him with all we have, all we are—yes, even the most cherished things in our spiritual experience—and we make known to him:

> Lord, I am willing to let go all of this for you: not just for your work, not for your children, not for anything else at all, but altogether and only for yourself!

Oh, to be wasted! It is a blessed thing to be wasted for the Lord. So many who have been prominent in the Christian world know nothing of this. Many of us have been used to the full—have been used, I would say, too much—but we do not know what it means to be *wasted on God*. We like to be always "on the go": the Lord would sometimes prefer to have us in prison. We think in terms of apostolic journeys: God dares to put his greatest ambassadors in chains.

But thanks be unto God, which always leadeth us in triumph in Christ, and maketh manifest through us the savor of his knowledge in every place (2 Cor. 2:14).

And the house was filled with the odor of the ointment (John 12:3).

The Lord grant us grace that we may learn how to please him. When, like Paul, we make this our supreme aim (2 Cor. 5:9), the Gospel will have achieved its end.

The Normal Christian Life

The text of this book is set in Goudy Old Style and Goudy Small Caps
with Woodtype Ornaments.

Typeset in Corel Ventura Publisher.

Preface to Hendrickson Christian Classics edition by Patricia Klein.

Copyediting, interior design, and production by
Publication Resources, Inc., of Ipswich, MA.
www.pubresources.com